RAND NATIONAL DEFENSE RESEA...

Programs Addressing Psychological Health and Resilience in the U.S. Department of Homeland Security

Carrie M. Farmer, Katie Whipkey, Margaret Chamberlin

Prepared for the Department of Homeland Security

Approved for public release; distribution unlimited

For more information on this publication, visit www.rand.org/t/RR1952

Library of Congress Cataloging-in-Publication Data is available for this publication.
ISBN: 978-1-9774-0197-7

Published by the RAND Corporation, Santa Monica, Calif.
© Copyright 2019 RAND Corporation
RAND® is a registered trademark.

Support RAND
Make a tax-deductible charitable contribution at
www.rand.org/giving/contribute

www.rand.org

Preface

U.S. Department of Homeland Security (DHS) employees support the department's vital mission of keeping the nation secure and are tasked with preventing terrorist attacks, securing the nation's borders, responding to natural disasters, and many other critical duties. Due to the nature of these jobs, many DHS employees face a range of work-related stressors that may put them at risk for developing psychological health problems. In response, DHS has developed and implemented a number of programs designed to promote resilience, offer peer support, and prevent psychological health problems among its staff.

Most of these programs are administered by the component agencies within DHS; however, there is no central repository of information about the nature of these programs, their program elements, or their effectiveness. To address this gap, the DHS Office of Health Affairs asked the RAND Corporation to describe the evidence base for workplace psychological health programs and identify existing programs that address psychological health, peer support, and resilience across DHS components. This report presents the findings from that analysis, which will be of interest not only to the DHS Office of Health Affairs but also to other government offices responsible for employee health and well-being.

This research was sponsored by the DHS Office of Health Affairs and conducted within the Forces and Resources Policy Center of the RAND National Defense Research Institute, a federally funded research and development center sponsored by the Office of the Secretary of Defense, the Joint Staff, the Unified Combatant Commands, the Navy, the Marine Corps, the defense agencies, and the defense Intelligence Community.

For more information on the RAND Forces and Resources Policy Center, see www.rand.org/nsrd/ndri/centers/frp or contact the director (contact information is provided on the webpage).

Contents

Figures and Tables

Figures

Tables

Summary

The U.S. Department of Homeland Security (DHS) was created in the aftermath of the September 11, 2001, terrorist attacks from all or part of 22 existing federal departments and agencies to oversee and coordinate a national strategy to protect the country from terrorism and to prevent future attacks. DHS currently employs more than 230,000 people who serve in different capacities across the department's operational components to prevent terrorism, secure and manage U.S. borders, enforce and administer immigration laws, safeguard and secure cyberspace, and ensure resilience to disasters. In carrying out these responsibilities, many DHS employees face considerable work-related stressors or are exposed to potentially traumatic events. The consequences could include job dissatisfaction, burnout, or psychological health problems, such as anxiety, depression, posttraumatic stress disorder, or substance use disorders. In 2012, the U.S. Government Accountability Office found evidence for increased stress among DHS employees and reported lower job satisfaction and lower engagement among DHS than the average of all other federal agencies based on data from the 2011 Federal Employee Viewpoint Survey.

The unique organizational structure of DHS and differences in the number and type of employees in each of its components have resulted in a support system that includes both DHS-wide programs and component-specific programs to help promote resilience and engagement among employees and prevent psychological health problems that can result from long-term stress and exposure to trauma. However, little is known about the nature and effectiveness of these programs. The

DHS Office of Health Affairs (OHA), which has shared responsibility with the Office of the Chief Human Capital Officer (OCHCO) for the overall well-being of the DHS workforce, asked the RAND Corporation to identify and inventory existing DHS programs that address psychological health, peer support, and resilience; to highlight gaps in existing programs relative to recommended practice; and to develop recommendations for new initiatives or for expanding or replicating existing evidence-based programs to support other DHS components.[1]

To support this effort, we conducted a series of interviews with subject-matter experts and DHS program managers to identify the psychological health risks faced by DHS employees, approaches to mitigating those risks, and existing programs across DHS that address psychological health. We also reviewed the research literature on key approaches to addressing psychological health that have been adopted by workforces similar to those of DHS components, including law enforcement, emergency medical services, and military personnel. We evaluated the evidence base for each approach to assess the level of certainty that a given intervention will have a net benefit for the population receiving it, with the goal of identifying the most appropriate interventions to meet the needs of DHS component employees.

Evaluation of Workplace Approaches to Increasing Resilience and Reducing Psychological Health Problems Among Employees

Overall, the evidence supporting commonly adopted workplace interventions to increase resilience and support psychological health was sparse, perhaps as a result of the newness of this field or the relative infrequency of traumatic events and ethical concerns related to conducting research on those exposed to such events. We adapted a metric developed by the U.S. Preventive Services Task Force (2013) to classify

---

[1]   This report was completed in November 2017. In December 2017, OHA functions were reorganized under OCHCO and the Countering Weapons of Mass Destruction Office. This report reflects the structure and functions of OHA before this reorganization.

the quality of the available evidence for each program type and the certainty of a net benefit as high, moderate, or low based on this evidence.

None of the interventions examined met the criteria for high certainty of a net benefit. Only five rose to the level of moderate certainty: (1) employee assistance programs (EAPs), (2) short-term counseling (for civilian populations only), (3) commercial resilience training programs (for civilian populations only), (4) psychological first aid, and (5) mental health first aid. All others had a low certainty of net benefit; however, in some cases, these approaches were either quite new or had shown promise for a subset of individuals (e.g., demonstrated effectiveness in civilian but not military populations). Table S.1 summarizes the interventions and the results of our evaluation.

Table S.1
Summary of Findings on Workplace Approaches to Promoting Resilience and Preventing Psychological Health Problems

Intervention	Purpose	Certainty of Positive Net Impact Based on Available Evidence
EAPs	Strategic guidance, support, and consultation offered internally to an organization or through an external provider to assist with personal or family issues	Moderate
Short-term counseling	Brief, solution-focused counseling to address general conditions of living and issues specific to the individual, such as stress management, adjustment challenges (e.g., reassignment, geographical moves), interpersonal problems, financial or employment issues, and grief and loss	Low-moderate
Self-care	Activities to nurture the self and promote well-being, such as meditation, mindfulness practice, moderate exercise, journaling, taking deliberate breaks from work or home tasks, participating in meaningful activities, or limiting unnecessary exposure to trauma	Low
Resilience training	Intervention before a problem appears, including educational programming or training on risk, strategies to manage stress and other risk factors, and recognizing warning signs of a developing problem	Low overall but moderate for commercial training programs for civilian populations

Table S.1—Continued

Intervention	Purpose	Certainty of Positive Net Impact Based on Available Evidence
Peer support	Peer-based intervention to help individuals respond to stress, including training for peer supporters to connect affected individual with resources or to provide case management support, education, or counseling	Low
Critical incident stress management	Acute crisis response, sometimes including pre-crisis and post-crisis components	Low
Critical incident stress debriefing	Structured, small-group acute crisis debriefing, either formal or informal, within 72 hours of event	Low; contraindicated
Psychological first aid	Response to individual psychological needs resulting from a disaster or traumatic event	Moderate
Stress first aid	Response to individual psychological needs resulting from job-related stress or traumatic events	Low
Mental health first aid	Response to individual needs of a person developing a mental health condition or having a mental health crisis	Moderate

Overview of DHS Programs to Address Employee Psychological Health

Through our interviews, we identified psychological health programs as of February 2017 in OHA and seven DHS operational components: U.S. Customs and Border Protection, the Federal Emergency Management Agency, U.S. Immigration and Customs Enforcement, Federal Law Enforcement Training Centers, the Transportation Security Administration, U.S. Citizenship and Immigration Services, and the U.S. Secret Service. Our study focused specifically on programs for preventing nonclinical psychological health issues (e.g., coping with stress, building resilience) and providing care (e.g., access to on-site mental health care providers, peer support, response to traumatic incidents). We did not include programs specifically targeting suicide, substance use, work-life balance, workplace violence, or health and wellness, which are informed by different sets of research. We also did not include programs in the U.S. Coast Guard. Finally, we note that it was not possible to conduct interviews with personnel at every location housing a given program, employees who participated in the programs described in this report, or DHS or component leadership. As a result, our findings do not represent a comprehensive account of perceptions regarding the function, purpose, and future of psychological health programs in individual components or across DHS.

DHS-Wide Programs

The Behavioral Health Branch (BHB) of OHA was established to address behavioral health matters, including resilience and suicidality. BHB uses an operational framework based on a health and wellness continuum, with an emphasis on evidence-based practices to advance health and well-being at individual and systemic levels. BHB focuses on both primary and secondary prevention, with initiatives aimed at reducing occupational stress and increasing resilience. It also supports component agencies in addressing the psychological health of their workforces.

Each DHS component agency offers an EAP that provides short-term counseling, access to 24-hour phone support, and some form of financial advice, general health and wellness information, support for life challenges, and other services. In some components, EAP providers play a prominent role in critical incident response. In others, these providers play a supportive role in responding to critical or traumatic incidents, if requested.

Component-Specific Programs

Individual DHS components provide a variety of services to their employees to address psychological health and promote resilience. Through our interviews, we identified existing component-level programs and categorized them according to the type of service they provided: peer support, critical or traumatic incident response, or resilience training. We also identified programs in development and related initiatives that components are pursuing to support the psychological health of their employees.

We found that most components had peer-support programs in place or in development—the Federal Emergency Management Agency was the exception—and these programs varied in terms of size, the amount and type training provided to peer supporters, and reporting requirements. A few components also provided short-term counseling and guidance on self-care as part of their EAPs. Finally, most offered some type of resilience training, but the focus of these programs varied.

Four of the DHS-wide or component-specific program types had a moderate or low-moderate certainty of having a positive net impact on participants: EAPs, short-term counseling, resilience training, and psychological first aid. As noted earlier, the level of certainty was determined from a review of the available literature, which is limited or lacks rigor for many types of interventions. It is unclear whether DHS programs using interventions with a low level of certainty of positive net impact have a positive impact in the context of DHS.

Recommendations

DHS employees are the front line for ensuring the safety and security of the United States. These jobs are inherently stressful, and some DHS employees risk exposure to emotional or traumatic events. To improve employees' psychological well-being, DHS must respond to their specific psychological health needs and concerns, as well as measure the effectiveness of existing programs that address psychological health. Our study suggests that the evidence base for most workplace psychological health interventions is limited due to a paucity of high-quality studies. While a peer-support program and other resilience initiatives may add nominal value and improve employee well-being overall, ensuring that these programs are both effective and beneficial to employees is paramount. The following recommendations provide a way forward for building on the current momentum with a focus on helping DHS determine whether its investments in these programs are achieving their desired outcomes for the department, its employees, and their families.

Recommendation 1. Ensure That All DHS Employees Have Access to Psychological Health Support

Given consistent findings of low morale among DHS employees and the work-related stressors they face, DHS should ensure that all employees have access to psychological health support when needed. It should also consider providing access to a DHS-trained licensed mental health care provider in each operational component.

Recommendation 2. Ensure That There Are Clear Policies for Peer-Support Programs in All Operational Components

Formal policies should outline all duties that peer supporters can and cannot perform, what training is required for performing those duties, what peer supporters can and cannot be held accountable for in their role, the resources in place to assist peer supporters, and the management plan and chain of command for peer supporters within the component. DHS should also ensure that peer supporters receive effective training, including refresher training at regular intervals.

Recommendation 3. Replace Formal Debriefing with a First-Aid Model

Although debriefing is sometimes used in law enforcement and other workplace contexts, the evidence does not support its continued use. Either stress first aid or psychological first aid would be an appropriate alternative that is supported by evidence.

Recommendation 4. Optimize Management of Psychological Health Programs Across DHS

DHS is a large, complex organization, and, as we discuss in this report, there have been numerous efforts across the department to address the psychological health of employees. To ensure that these efforts are coordinated and to optimize the management of its portfolio of programs, DHS should develop mechanisms for ensuring consistency across psychological health programs and components. Improved communication and regular collaboration among program managers and leadership would help streamline and unify these efforts. Such an approach could also help components learn from one another and increase ownership and responsibility for employee well-being, psychological health, and job satisfaction. In addition, DHS should conduct a psychological health needs assessment prior to developing new programs. Finally, this report provides a "snapshot" of programs identified in selected DHS components as of February 2017. Inevitably, these programs will change over time as funding, priorities, and staffing changes in components. DHS should develop a mechanism for sustaining a list of all psychological health programs across the department.

Recommendation 5. Build Evaluation into Psychological Health Programs

Without a systematic process for evaluation, untested programs could be a poor investment of resources or inadvertently result in harm to those who participate in them. None of the programs identified in this study had been formally evaluated by an external organization, and DHS had evaluated only six programs in two components. To address this gap, DHS should develop criteria to assess program effectiveness and encourage components to collect consistent data on their programs and implement quality improvement processes to address programs that are not meeting their goals. The data collected should not include any personally identifiable information to ensure the confidentiality of the employees who use the program's services. For large or critical programs, it may be appropriate for DHS to contract with an independent external evaluator.

Acknowledgments

We gratefully acknowledge the support of our project monitors in the DHS Office of Health Affairs, Mary Good and CAPT Scott Salvatore. We also thank our points of contact in U.S. Customs and Border Protection, the Federal Emergency Management Agency, Immigration and Customs Enforcement, the Federal Law Enforcement Training Centers, the Transportation Security Administration, U.S. Citizenship and Immigration Services, and the U.S. Secret Service who agreed to participate in our interviews and provide information about ongoing psychological health programs in these component agencies.

We appreciate the comments provided by our reviewers, Rajeev Ramchand and Patricia Watson. Their constructive critiques were addressed as part of RAND's rigorous quality assurance process and improved this report. We thank Lauren Skrabala for her editorial assistance. Finally, we are grateful for the support and assistance of Laura Pavlock-Albright as we conducted this study and prepared this report.

Abbreviations

AMO	Air and Marine Operations
BHB	Behavioral Health Branch
CBP	U.S. Customs and Border Protection
CISD	critical incident stress debriefing
CISM	critical incident stress management
COSFA	Combat and Operational Stress First Aid
CSF2	Comprehensive Soldier and Family Fitness
DHS	U.S. Department of Homeland Security
EAP	employee assistance program
FAMS	Federal Air Marshal Service
FEMA	Federal Emergency Management Agency
FEVS	Federal Employee Viewpoint Survey
FLETC	Federal Law Enforcement Training Centers
GAO	U.S. Government Accountability Office
GTO	Getting To Outcomes
HQ	headquarters

ICE	U.S. Immigration and Customs Enforcement
IOM	Institute of Medicine
ICISF	International Critical Incident Stress Foundation, Inc.
MHFA	mental health first aid
OCHCO	Office of the Chief Human Capital Officer
OFO	Office of Field Operations
OHA	Office of Health Affairs
PFA	psychological first aid
PTSD	posttraumatic stress disorder
SFA	stress first aid
TRiM	Trauma Risk Management
TSA	Transportation Security Administration
USCIS	U.S. Citizenship and Immigration Services
USSS	U.S. Secret Service
USPSTF	U.S. Preventive Services Task Force
VA	U.S. Department of Veterans Affairs

CHAPTER ONE

Background

The U.S. Department of Homeland Security (DHS) employs more than 230,000 people who are responsible for fulfilling the department's mission to "ensure a homeland that is safe, secure, and resilient against terrorism and other hazards" (DHS, 2016). DHS employees work in different capacities across the department's operational components to prevent terrorism, secure and manage U.S. borders, enforce and administer immigration laws, safeguard and secure cyberspace, and ensure resilience to disasters. In carrying out these responsibilities, many DHS employees face considerable work-related stressors. The U.S. Government Accountability Office (GAO) reported in 2012 that DHS employees had lower job satisfaction and lower engagement than the average of all other federal agencies, according to data from the 2011 Federal Employee Viewpoint Survey (FEVS), which is administered by the Office of Personnel Management (GAO, 2012). DHS has developed and implemented a number of programs with the goals of promoting resilience and morale among employees and preventing psychological health problems.

Most DHS psychological health programs are administered by and within the department's operational components and are tailored to meet the needs of component employees; however, little is known about the nature and effectiveness of these programs. The DHS Office of Health Affairs (OHA) has shared responsibility with the Office of the Chief Human Capital Officer (OCHCO) for the overall well-being of the DHS workforce and, as such, requires information about existing programs to inform decisions about additional programming and resource allocation.[1] To address this need, OHA asked the RAND Corporation to identify and inventory existing DHS programs that address psychological health, peer support, and resilience; to identify gaps in existing programs relative to recommended practice; and to develop recommendations for new initiatives or for expanding or replicating existing evidence-based programs to support other DHS components.

Methods

We conducted a literature review and a series of interviews with subject-matter experts and DHS program managers to identify the psychological health risks faced by DHS employees, approaches to mitigating those risks, and existing programs across DHS that address psychological health.[2] We focused on DHS programs for preventing nonclinical psychological health issues (e.g., coping with stress, building resilience) and providing care (e.g., access to on-site mental health care providers, peer support, response to traumatic incidents). We did not include programs specifically targeting suicide or substance use. While these are of course important, they address more serious clinical behavioral health problems that require a different set of resources based on a different research base. We also did not include programs addressing work-life balance, workplace violence, or health and wellness, since such programs also require a different research base and were not identified by DHS as key areas of focus. We identified programs in place as of February 2017 in OHA and seven operational components: U.S. Customs and Border Protection (CBP), the Federal Emergency Management Agency (FEMA), Federal Law Enforcement Training Centers (FLETC), U.S. Immigration and Customs Enforcement (ICE),

---

[1] This report was completed in November 2017. In December 2017, OHA functions were reorganized under OCHCO and the Countering Weapons of Mass Destruction Office. This report reflects OHA's structure and functions before this reorganization.

[2] The study was reviewed by RAND's Human Subjects Protection Committee and was determined not to be research involving human subjects, thus not requiring further review.

the Transportation Security Administration (TSA), U.S. Citizenship and Immigration Services (USCIS), and the U.S. Secret Service (USSS). These operational components were identified with input from OHA. We did not include programs in the U.S. Coast Guard, but they have been described in previous RAND work (Weinick et al., 2011).

We identified relevant literature by first reviewing recent reports on the DHS workforce and the subjects of resilience and psychological health by GAO and the Institute of Medicine (IOM), as well as completed and ongoing related research at RAND. We then examined the peer-reviewed academic literature on approaches to preventing psychological health problems. From these sources, as well as a preliminary understanding of the types of programs currently available across DHS and previous RAND research on the types of psychological health programs offered in other U.S. government organizations (Weinick et al., 2011), we identified seven key approaches to addressing workplace psychological health: self-care, resilience training, employee assistance programs (EAPs), short-term counseling, peer support, critical incident stress management/debriefing, and psychological/stress/mental health first aid.

Next, we searched the literature to identify studies of the effectiveness of these approaches using a combination of search terms for each approach (e.g., peer support) and "evidence," "evaluation," or "effectiveness." We also searched for examples of each approach in practice, particularly in settings that were similar to DHS. Our literature search focused on peer-reviewed articles and gray literature published since 2007, though we did scan earlier articles and solicited recommendations from subject-matter experts to ensure that we identified any landmark studies. After we identified relevant studies, we synthesized the information around each typology (e.g., self-care, peer support) to summarize the evidence on the effectiveness of the practice. We adapted a metric developed by the U.S. Preventive Services Task Force (USPSTF, 2013) to classify the quality of the available evidence for each program type. We classified the certainty of a net benefit of an intervention as high, moderate, or low based on this evidence (see Table 1.1).

Table 1.1
USPSTF Levels of Certainty Regarding Net Benefit as Adapted for This Study

Level of Certainty[a]	Description
High	The available evidence usually includes consistent results from well-designed, well-conducted studies of representative populations. These studies assess the effects of the preventive service on psychological health or resilience outcomes.
Moderate	The available evidence is sufficient to determine the effects of the service on psychological health or resilience outcomes, but confidence in the estimate is constrained by such factors as • the number, size, or quality of studies • inconsistency of findings across studies • limited generalizability of findings. As more information becomes available, the magnitude or direction of the observed effect could change, and this change may be large enough to alter the conclusion.
Low	The available evidence is insufficient to assess effects on psychological health or resilience outcomes. Evidence is insufficient for one of the following reasons: • limited number or size of studies • significant flaws in study design or methods • inconsistency of findings across studies • findings are not generalizable • lack of information on important psychological health or resilience outcomes. More information may allow estimation of effects on psychological health or resilience outcomes.

SOURCE: Adapted from USPSTF, 2013. Official levels of certainty as of July 2012.

[a] *Certainty* is defined as likelihood that an assessment of a service's net benefit (benefit minus potential harm) is correct. USPSTF assigns a certainty level based on the nature of the overall available evidence to assess the net benefit of a preventive service. We have adapted this scale for our use in exploring interventions to improve psychological health or resilience.

We conducted interviews with 23 staff in OHA and the selected DHS components who were responsible for programs addressing psychological heath, including EAP managers and clinicians, peer-support program managers, directors of component resiliency programs, and other employees who were knowledgeable about psychological health in their components. We did not interview component agency leadership, law enforcement officers, or union representatives, who may have provided different perspectives. Our study point of contact in OHA identified relevant personnel in component agencies; in several instances, we conducted additional interviews with individuals recommended by the initial component point of contact. We asked interviewees to describe their role, the psychological health risks faced by employees in their component, and current programs to prevent psychological health problems, identify psychological health needs, and connect employees with needed care. We asked additional questions about each identified program, including the purpose and activities of each program, program participation and outreach (i.e., program size, budget, and funding), whether the program had been evaluated, and major prior and future changes to the program. All interviewees had the opportunity to review the information we collected and to correct or clarify the details.

Overview of the U.S. Department of Homeland Security

In response to the September 11, 2001, terrorist attacks, President George W. Bush established the White House Office of Homeland Security to oversee and coordinate a national strategy to protect the country from terrorism and to prevent future attacks. The office, which comprised all or part of 22 federal departments and agencies, became a Cabinet-level department (DHS) in 2002. DHS is organized into headquarters-level offices and operational component agencies that report directly to the Secretary of Homeland Security. Figure 1.1 shows its organizational structure at the time of our research in November 2017.

Each operational component has a specific mission that is integral to the wider mission of DHS (see Table 1.2). Each component also has autonomy in determining the means used to carry out its mission, and, as such, differs considerably from other components in terms of the number and type of employees.

Figure 1.1
DHS Organizational Structure

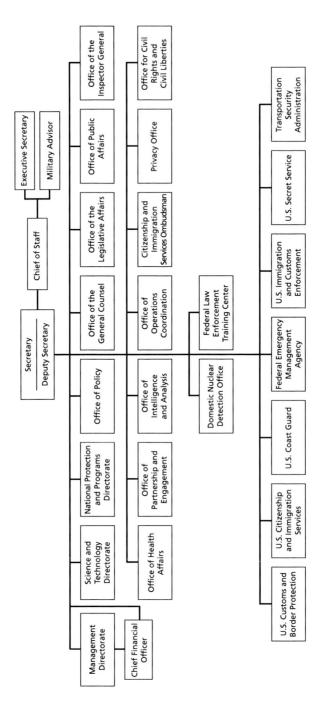

SOURCE: DHS, 2017.
NOTE: The figure shows the organizational structure of DHS at the time this research was conducted.

Table 1.2
Mission and Size of Selected DHS Component Agencies

Component	Official Mission Statement	Full-Time Employees (as of 2016)
CBP	"To safeguard U.S. borders thereby protecting the public from dangerous people and materials while enhancing the Nation's global economic competitiveness by enabling legitimate trade and travel."	59,054
FEMA	"FEMA's mission is to support our citizens and first responders to ensure that as a nation we work together to build, sustain and improve our capability to prepare for, protect against, respond to, recover from and mitigate hazards."	9,153
FLETC	"FLETC's mission is to train all those who protect the homeland."	1,211
ICE	"U.S. Immigration and Customs Enforcement (ICE) enforces federal laws governing border control, customs, trade and immigration to promote homeland security and public safety."	19,217
TSA	"Protect the nation's transportation systems to ensure freedom of movement for people and commerce."	51,345
USCIS	"USCIS secures America's promise as a nation of immigrants by providing accurate and useful information to our customers, granting immigration and citizenship benefits, promoting an awareness and understanding of citizenship, and ensuring the integrity of our immigration system."	15,247
USSS	Investigative mission: "[T]he agency's investigative mission has evolved from enforcing counterfeiting laws to safeguarding the payment and financial systems of the United States from a wide range of financial and computer-based crimes." Protective mission: "The Secret Service is recognized for the physical protection it provides to the nation's highest elected leaders, visiting foreign dignitaries, facilities and major events."	6,473

SOURCES: Official mission statements from component agencies' websites (CBP, 2016; FEMA, 2017; FLETC, undated; ICE, 2017; TSA, undated; USCIS, 2018; USSS, undated[a], undated[b]). Data on the number of full-time employees in 2016 from the Office of Personnel Management's FedScope database as of February 2017.

Organization of This Report

In Chapter Two, we describe the types of psychological health risks DHS employees may face and the impact of stressors on job performance. Chapter Three describes the evidence for various approaches to increasing workforce resilience and reducing the incidence of psychological health problems. In Chapter Four, we present our findings on DHS-wide and component-specific programs addressing psychological health. (A complete list of these programs can be found in the appendix.) Chapter Five concludes the report with a summary of our findings and recommendations.

CHAPTER TWO

Overview of Work-Related Stressors and Psychological Health Risks Among DHS Employees

As an IOM study for OHA concluded in 2013, "The nature of the DHS work environment is inherently stressful, and the responsibilities can weigh heavily on DHS employees at every level and in every facet of the organization" (IOM, 2013, p. 4) These stressors and their resulting effects on employee job satisfaction have been documented in recent GAO reports as well, and our interviews with employee wellness and psychological health program representatives across DHS also echoed those findings. In this chapter, we provide a brief overview of the types of stressors and psychological health risks faced by DHS employees, as well as the impact of these stressors on job performance.

Work-Related Stressors and Psychological Health Risks

In 2012, GAO reported that DHS employees had 4.5-percent lower job satisfaction and 7-percent lower engagement than the average of all other federal agencies (see GAO, 2012). Employees in some DHS components, such as TSA, displayed particularly low morale. DHS employee job satisfaction decreased an additional 7 percent by 2013, outpacing the government-wide decrease of 4 percent over the same period and further widening the morale gap between DHS and the rest of the federal service sector (Maurer, 2013). A November 2016 report by the DHS Office of the Inspector General suggested that the department's low FEVS scores may have been due to a lack of "clear and consistent guidance" for employees, poor communication between high- and lower-level of staff, and inadequate training (Roth, 2016).

The 2013 IOM report mentioned at the beginning of this chapter examined the stressors contributing to a less engaged and less resilient DHS workforce, identifying two main categories of work-related stress for DHS employees: institutional or job function stressors that are common across components and job-related emotional or traumatic stressors that are unique to specific divisions within components (IOM, 2013).

Institutional or Job Function Stressors

DHS is a complex organization. As a consequence of its formation from multiple organizations in 2002, it has struggled to integrate its various components and develop a cohesive organizational culture (IOM, 2013). The 2013 IOM report and our interviewees identified a number of stressors that DHS employees face as a result of the department's structure. For example, DHS employees who provided public comments to IOM reported frustration with a lack of clarity about roles and responsibilities. These employees cited unclear expectations, insufficient written guidance, significant responsibility without appropriate support, unclear feedback on job performance, and impossibly tight deadlines (IOM, 2013). In our interviews, representatives from several DHS components noted common problems with job mismatches: Staff are sometimes placed in positions for which they have not been formally trained or have skill sets that do not match the job description. This lack of job clarity and preparation can lead to anxiety about the ability to fulfill the needs of the position, concerns about job security, and ambiguous paths for professional growth, as training and continuing education are not always efficient or even available. The IOM report and several of our interviewees also described stress resulting from a perceived "leadership vacuum," in which supervisors and managers are inadequately trained and prepared to provide guidance to employees and enact a job appraisal system.[1] The consequences of such a situation can take a variety of forms, including micromanagement, disconnection between middle management and leadership, abrupt changes in work direction when leadership changes, and favoritism.

---

[1]   Interviews with CBP, FEMA, and ICE staff, December 2016–January 2017.

Many DHS employees work long hours, and some job functions require employees to be available around the clock to respond to crises. Certain roles (e.g., analysts in the national operations center and related component-level operations centers) even require full-time staffing around the clock. These types of jobs require shift schedules, and, according to the IOM report, these schedules can change frequently and can contribute to burnout, poor sleep, and, ultimately, poor performance (IOM, 2013). All the component representatives we interviewed highlighted working long hours, often resulting in extensive overtime, as a routine stressor for employees. Many noted that the long hours caused sleeping problems for employees, leading to increased stress levels.[2] These interviewees also frequently cited personal relationship stressors resulting from extensive travel and long working hours.

Finally, some component interviewees reported that employees can face stressors related to an uncertain political climate in terms of job security, tasks, and public exposure.[3] Public attitudes toward law enforcement may compound such stressors. A national survey by the CATO Institute found deep partisan and racial divides in perceptions of the police (Ekins, 2016). Other studies have confirmed such divides (Maxson, Hennigan, and Sloane, 2003). In a recent Pew study, 86 percent of police officers reported that their jobs are harder now than before, potentially due to high-profile fatal encounters that have aggravated tensions between police and citizens. Approximately half of officers reported frustration with their jobs, two-thirds had experienced verbal abuse from community members, and the majority had serious concerns about their safety while on the job. They also cited strong skepticism that the public understands the risks they face (Morin et al., 2017). Some DHS law enforcement personnel have similar problems with public perception, though this varies significantly by component. For example, while the U.S. Coast Guard workforce is widely viewed as

---

[2] Interviews with CBP, FEMA, TSA, USCIS, and USSS staff, December 2016–January 2017.

[3] Interviews with ICE and USSS staff, December 2016–February 2017.

heroic and effective, TSA personnel are often perceived poorly despite performing their jobs effectively (IOM, 2013).

Emotional or Traumatic Stressors

Approximately 50 percent of DHS employees are law enforcement personnel (IOM, 2013). Law enforcement professionals face unique stressors because of both the inherent risk of the work they do and the significantly increased rate of exposure to potentially traumatizing events (Kureczka, 1996; Gershon et al., 2009; Colwell et al., 2011). A 2012 survey asked nearly 1,000 police officers to rate their perceived levels of stress for numerous common law enforcement tasks. Pursuing suspects (either by car or on foot) and witnessing a traumatic event prompted the highest level of perceived stress. Overall, perceived stress was highest for tasks inherent to law enforcement work (e.g., serving a warrant, physical altercations), as opposed to routine, nonemergency work (e.g., completing reports, attending meetings) (Korre et al., 2014). DHS component interviewees (from CBP, FLETC, ICE, TSA, and USSS) reported that their employees faced common law enforcement–specific stressors, such as safety concerns, perceptions of being a target, and exposure to violence and trauma.

In some divisions of DHS, employees may face other unique stressors. For example, many employees in operational components work in austere environments or are exposed to dangerous and traumatic events as a function of their day-to-day work (IOM, 2013). Employees in the USCIS Refugee, Asylum and International Operations Directorate process asylum seekers and face stress associated with hearing upsetting life stories, encountering people in devastating situations, and determining the fate of these individuals.[4] FEMA employees experience disasters firsthand and are exposed for an extended period to loss of life and property.[5] ICE employees who work in that agency's child exploitation and human trafficking divisions may experience psychological health problems from daily exposure to these crimes.[6]

---

[4] Interview with USCIS staff, January 2017.

[5] Interview with FEMA staff, December 2016.

[6] Interview with ICE staff, December 2016.

Secondary Trauma

Some DHS employees may experience psychological health problems resulting from indirect exposure to a traumatic event, such as talking to those who have experienced a traumatic event (Baird and Kracen, 2006; Palm, Polusny, and Follette, 2004). Numerous studies have found that people who directly experience trauma are more likely to experience psychological symptoms than those who indirectly experience it (Zimering et al., 2006; Salston and Figley, 2003; Palm, Polusny, and Follette, 2004), but there is some risk for those who are indirectly exposed (Elwood et al., 2011). While there is not consensus as to whether exposure to secondary trauma has an adverse impact, studies of law enforcement professionals, psychotherapists, clinicians, and relief workers have generally found an increased incidence of psychological symptoms subsequent to indirect exposure to trauma, though some findings indicate that symptoms are not clinically significant (Adams, Figley, and Boscarino, 2008; Figley, 2002; Zimering et al., 2006; Meffert et al., 2014). Generally, reactions to secondary trauma are similar to those of individuals who actually experienced the trauma, including recurring thoughts or imagery, detachment, avoidance, decreased motivation, anxiety, sleeping problems, and substance abuse (Palm, Polusny, and Follette, 2004; Baird and Kracen, 2006; Figley, 2002).

The research on the likelihood of experiencing secondary trauma has been mixed. A study of Australian internet child exploitation workers found that few investigators felt that the work was affecting them negatively, though many reported knowing former employees who left the profession due to its impact on their psychological health (Powell et al., 2014). Disaster relief workers, whose jobs are similar to those of some FEMA employees, have been found to have high rates of posttraumatic stress disorder (PTSD). Rescue workers in Greece during the European refugee crisis were found to have a 17-percent PTSD prevalence rate (Sifaki-Pistolla et al., 2017). In a study of trained relief workers at Ground Zero in New York City, nearly 5 percent met the criteria for PTSD, while 4 percent of people who were exposed to the terrorist attacks and aftermath only through television still experienced some degree of PTSD (Zimering et al., 2006). In another study, 65 percent of Oklahoma City bombing trauma workers experienced symptoms of PTSD (Figley, 2002; Wee and Myers, 2002). A meta-analysis of psychological health complaints by disaster volunteers found that familiarity with victims, severity of exposure, anxiety sensitivity, and lack of support post-disaster were significant contributors to complaints (Thormar et al., 2010). However, one study of a police special forces unit during both typical daily duty and a single high-stress event suggested that the routine work was more stressful (Garbarino et al., 2011).

Impact of Stress on Job Performance

Significant work-related stress can affect an individual's resilience, psychological health, and ability to make clear decisions. Studies of law enforcement officers and first responders have found a relationship between stress and increased distress, frequently measured through such symptoms as excessive alcohol consumption or diagnostic surveys for common mental health disorders, such as depression and PTSD (Ellrich and Baier, 2017; Benedek, Fullerton, and Ursano, 2007; Chopko, Palmieri, and Adams, 2013, 2016). Burnout can be a common outcome for individuals in high-stress fields (Awa, Plaumann, and Walter, 2010). Burnout is predominantly defined by three key components: emotional exhaustion, depersonalization (often characterized as cynicism), and reduced personal accomplishment. Employees who experience burnout are more likely to report psychological health problems, including anxiety, depression, and alcohol dependence (Bakker and Costa, 2014). In addition, there is evidence that occupational burnout may lead to secondary traumatic stress. A 2015 study employed a longitudinal approach to analyze this relationship in two samples of health professionals who worked with victims of trauma, one in the United States and one in Poland. In both samples, high occupational burnout at baseline was predictive of secondary trauma measured six months later (Shoji et al., 2015). Studies of the impact of stress on decisionmaking have found that stress not only impairs understanding of the logic behind a complex decision, but it also degrades the capacity for strategizing (Leder, Häusser, and Mojzisch, 2015). A review of the existing literature on stress and decisionmaking found that acute stress can enhance decision biases, increasing risky choices (Morgado, Sousa, and Cerqueira, 2015).

Conclusion

Understanding the potential effects of work-related stressors on employees can inform appropriate interventions to improve employees' psychological health and resilience. Based on our interviews with DHS component representatives and a review of previous studies, we identified institutional and job-related stressors that affect most DHS employees, as well as emotional or traumatic stressors that affect a subset of employees—namely, law enforcement personnel. In the next chapter, we describe several workplace approaches to improving psychological health and resilience and, for each, assess the evidence base and relevance to DHS.

CHAPTER THREE

Workplace Approaches to Increasing Resilience and Reducing Psychological Health Problems Among Employees

There are several strategies and interventions designed to prevent psychological health problems and improve resilience in the workplace. In this chapter, we describe seven common categories of psychological health approaches and weigh the evidence for their effectiveness using the USPSTF levels of certainty described in Chapter One (see Table 1.1). There is not a robust pool of evidence for these strategies, and prior studies vary widely in the types of effects studied and outcomes measured. Therefore, our review synthesized the key literature and specific studies, but we did not conduct a comprehensive meta-analysis for each of the seven categories or for psychological health interventions more broadly.

Employee Assistance Programs

EAPs are services provided to employees and their families by an employer that are designed to assist with personal or family issues. EAPs provide strategic guidance, support, and consultation on such topics as psychological health, substance abuse, financial wellness, legal concerns, and marital and parenting problems. They are designed to help employees stay effective on the job (Employee Assistance Trade Association, undated). EAPs are often contracted to an external provider but may also be run internally within an organization or as a hybrid of internal and external services. External vendors are often preferable because they are immediately implementable, often more cost-effective, and have lower legal liability. They may also foster increased employee trust in confidentiality assurances and separate employee services from the internal politics of an organization. Conversely, external EAPs may not be tailored to the specific needs of an organization or may have less accountability. Internal EAPs, on the other hand, may foster greater ownership and be more easily integrated into existing internal resources. However, they could also be expensive and risk employee confidentiality (Sharar, Pompe, and Attridge, 2013).

While EAPs are common—77 percent of firms in the United States offered one in 2014 (Matos and Galinsky, 2014)—evidence of their impact on employee psychological health is limited (Bennett et al., 2015). Most of the few studies have been conducted by EAP providers for promotional purposes and are potentially biased (Bennett et al., 2015). There is also little scientific research on the costs and benefits of these services (Lerner et al., 2013). Two studies have measured cost-effectiveness and found a significant cost savings. In one analysis of a workplace wellness program offered by a large company, reducing employees' health risks by increasing participation in the wellness program yielded a return on investment of six to one against health care costs associated with employee insurance plans (Berry, Mirabito, and Baun, 2010). Another study found large cost savings from increased productivity by integrating mental health care resources through the EAP (Loeppke, 2009). Although EAPs differ across organizations, they are widespread and commonly used; therefore, the level of certainty of a net benefit from EAP programs is moderate.

Short-Term Counseling

Short-term counseling is brief, solution-focused counseling designed to address general conditions of living and issues specific to the individual, including but not limited to stress management, adjustment challenges (e.g., reassignment, relocation), interpersonal problems, financial or employment issues, and grief and loss. This kind of brief counseling is conducted by a licensed mental health care provider and is aimed at preventing the development or exacerbation of mental health disorders that may limit functioning (Warner, Meisnere, and Denning, 2014).

Most EAPs offer this type of short-term counseling, generally providing up to six visits with a mental health care provider to address a particular issue. A systematic review of workplace counseling, including counseling provided through EAPs, suggested that counseling is generally effective in alleviating psychological health problems, has a significant impact on sickness absence, and has a moderate effect on attitudes toward work. However, the review noted methodological limitations in many of the studies (McLeod, 2010). Given these limitations, more research is needed to verify the effectiveness of short-term counseling for reducing psychological health problems among employees in civilian workplace settings. Based on the existing evidence, the level of certainty of a net benefit of short-term counseling among civilian populations is moderate.

In the U.S. Department of Defense, all active-duty, National Guard, and reserve members and their families can access confidential, free, short-term counseling sessions. Services are available from two sources: Military OneSource and the Military and Family Life Consultant program. Services, which include evidence-based problem-solving therapy and short-term counseling, are available to active-duty service members and families on or off military installations. In a 2010 evaluation of the Military and Family Life Consultant program using self-reported data collected from program participants, 98 percent of respondents reported that the counseling sessions helped them deal more effectively with their problems and that they would use the service again (U.S. Department of Defense, 2012). Nearly all participants (99 percent) reported that they received the type of counseling service they requested and would recommend it to a friend. A second study used data collected through the May 2010 Military Family Life Survey to evaluate the impact of Military OneSource on service members' spouses. Military OneSource's nonmedical counseling was the second most utilized source of counseling among spouses, and more than half reported that it was "very useful" (Defense Manpower Data Center, 2011). The weight of this evidence is significantly limited because both studies evaluated only program participants' reactions to the programs and did not evaluate resilience or psychological health outcomes. In short, the level of certainty of a net benefit from short-term counseling among military populations is low.

Self-Care

Self-care has been defined as "the practice of activities that individuals initiate and perform on their own behalf in maintaining life, health, and well-being" (Orem, 1991). These activities vary widely and are often specific to the individual. Some examples include meditation, mindfulness practice, moderate exercise, journaling, taking deliberate breaks from work or home tasks, participating in meaningful activities, or limiting unnecessary exposure to trauma (Adams, Figley, and Boscarino, 2008; Salston and Figley, 2003; Radey and Figley, 2007; Palm, Polusny, and Follette, 2004). Self-care nurtures the self and promotes well-being by enhancing self-awareness, self-efficacy, confidence, sense of purpose, and meaning and facilitates positive adaptation and cognitive transformation (Grafton, Gillespie, and Henderson, 2010). Self-care is often studied in conjunction with other resilience development and strengthening activities. In most studies, it is a minor component of a broader resilience intervention, so there is limited evidence of the impact of self-care specifically. However, it is commonly accepted and frequently recommended by practitioners in the physical and mental health fields, as well as for other purposes, such as recovery from substance and alcohol use disorders.

One example from the literature on self-care is a study that measured the impact of the introduction of a health enhancement program, in which self-care was the main component, on medical student psychological distress and quality of life. The study found that self-care, in the form of mindfulness-based stress management and lifestyle programs (e.g., journaling, educating, and then encouraging experimentation with other self-care activities) significantly reduced student stress levels, even during times of extreme stress, such as examinations. A limitation to this example is that the population studied may have been quite different from the DHS workforce. The study also lacked a true control group, as the health enhancement program was available to all students (Hassed et al., 2009). In a separate pilot study, self-care was used as a stress-reducing tool among psychiatrists, a population at risk for both routine and more acute stressful events. The study was small (only 37 participants), but it did employ a randomized controlled trial design with an intervention group and a control group. An evaluation found a statistically significant improvement in perceived stress, resilience, and self-efficacy in the intervention group (Mache et al., 2016). Both of these studies provide promising evidence but included only subjective measures of impact on resilience or stress, and neither study assessed any potential psychological health outcomes.

While the literature supporting the efficacy of self-care is limited, it is used in many resilience-building programs, and self-care is recommended by many practicing clinicians as a way to reduce stress. The level of certainty of a net benefit from self-care is low, but the level of risk is also quite low, leading to its frequent use in practice.

Resilience Training

Another strategy to increase resilience is to intervene before a problem appears. *Resilience* is generally defined as "the process of adapting well in the face of adversity, trauma, tragedy, threats or even significant sources of stress" (American Psychological Association, undated). Resilience education programming or training can disseminate information about risk, strategies to manage stress, and warning signs of a developing problem. There are commercial programs for promoting resilience that have demonstrated effectiveness in reducing both psychosocial and physical stress. One such program, Williams LifeSkills, was designed to reduce psychosocial problems that are associated with poor chronic disease outcomes (Williams and Williams, 2011). A second example, HardiTraining, was developed to promote hardiness among a more general audience (e.g., working adults) (Meadows, Miller, and Robson, 2015). While hardiness is not the same as resilience, a significant body of literature shows that they are strongly linked constructs (Connor, Davidson, and Lee, 2003; Agaibi and Wilson, 2005). There is evidence that HardiTraining effectively promoted self-reported hardiness and social support and decreased self-reported strain and illness severity in civilian populations (Maddi et al., 2009).

In civilian work settings, psychoeducational programs, such as stress inoculation training and acceptance commitment therapy, have been shown to reduce anxiety and improve performance under stress (Flaxman and Bond, 2010). There is also evidence that resilience training can have a positive effect on government employees. One example is a study conducted in the early 2000s to determine the efficacy of a specific worksite training program in a regional office of a large government agency. The study evaluated the program's impact on selected resilience qualities (self-esteem, locus of control, purpose in life, and interpersonal relations) and job satisfaction. Using random assignment to treatment and control groups, the study demonstrated a significant positive change in five of six resilience qualities for the group that received resilience training. (There was no positive change for job satisfaction.) No change was seen in the group that did not receive the training. The study did not go so far as to compare the two groups to determine the statistical significance of the results (Waite and Richardson, 2004). However, it does provide promising evidence for training as an approach to building resilience to the day-to-day stressors experienced by DHS employees.

A number of programs developed for military populations (e.g., the Air Force's Airman Resilience Training, the Army's Comprehensive Soldier and Family Fitness [CSF2]) were designed in whole or in part to promote resilience. Most military programs include strategies to strengthen at least one evidence-informed factor associated with resilience, such as positive thinking, behavioral control, and a positive command climate (Meredith et al., 2011), but methodologically strong evidence of these programs' effectiveness is scarce.

CSF2 is probably the most widespread ongoing intervention designed to increase resilience among soldiers and their families. Among the components of CSF2 is Master Resilience Training, which Army research has found to increase aspects of resilience, including adaptability and optimism (Harms et al., 2013). Unfortunately, there are no independent, peer-reviewed, published analyses of CSF2 (Steenkamp, Nash, and Litz, 2013). A study of the Comprehensive Airman Fitness program showed that it was positively linked to resilience across the Air Force. While this is a promising finding, the study was methodologically limited, and its results should be considered preliminary (Bowen, 2016). A 2015 RAND study of Comprehensive Airman Fitness examined the constructs guiding the program and resilience interventions currently used by the Air Force. One such intervention was Airman Resilience Training, an educational briefing designed to improve airmen's psychological reactions to the stress they face during and after deployment and to encourage the use of mental health services by those who could benefit (Meadows, Miller, and Robson, 2015). Unfortunately, the study focused only on existing programs and did not evaluate their effectiveness (Robson, 2014). A separate RAND study found that airmen who received the Airman Resilience Training intervention during deployment and reintegration did not perceive it to be useful (Gonzalez et al., 2014).

Outside the military context, one study examined the impact of resilience training provided to a randomly assigned group of trainees at a police academy. After 18 months on the force, all members of the graduating class were evaluated. Those in the treatment group showed statistically significantly reduced stress responses in terms of both physical health and self-identified psychological well-being (Arnetz et al., 2013). A systematic review of 14 studies that examined the impact of work-based resilience training interventions found some beneficial effects on individuals, such as increased subjective well-being, enhanced psychosocial functioning, and improved workplace performance. However, the studies lacked coherence in design and robustness, and resilience was defined and assessed differently among the studies; therefore, they do not provide conclusive findings on the effectiveness of resilience training content and format (Robertson et al., 2015).

Although these studies demonstrate improvement of one or more evidence-informed factors associated with resilience, there is no current evidence to support the effectiveness of resilience programs in preventing future psychological health problems (Meredith et al., 2011). However, resilience programs differ greatly, and the level of certainty of their effectiveness is difficult to assess. For military and law enforcement resilience training, the level of certainty of a net benefit is low on the whole. For commercial training programs, the level of certainty is moderate. Studies of those programs are well designed, and the results are consistent, but they are limited in their generalizability to the DHS workforce.

Peer Support

Peers can serve as an important resource for helping individuals respond to stress. Programs that train individuals to provide support to their peers can take a number of forms, such as training for peer supporters to connect the affected individual with resources or to provide case management support, education, or counseling. While there is very little research on peer support for resilience building, it is considered an evidence-based best practice in other settings. Specific peer-based facilitation interventions for managing chronic diseases (Druss et al., 2010), preventing eating disorders among college undergraduates (Stice et al., 2013), and supporting weight loss (Pullen et al., 2008) have all demonstrated positive effects. In addition, a review of the literature on peer support in mental health services found that peer supporters have the potential to reduce hospital admissions among those they serve. That study also concluded that peer support could have a positive impact on the lives of individuals with mental illness (Repper and Carter, 2011). An additional systematic review of the effectiveness of peer-based interventions found evidence for positive changes in health behaviors. However, much of this research focused on physical health behavior change (e.g., smoking cessation, physical activity) (Webel et al., 2010).

A peer-support model focused on psychological risk assessment used by the British military may be a better model for DHS. The Trauma Risk Management (TRiM) program is a proactive peer-group model of psychological risk assessment that has been used by the Royal Marines for more than ten years. There have been least two studies of TRiM's effectiveness in reducing levels of psychological distress. First, prior to its implementation, the Royal Navy conducted a cluster randomized controlled trial of TRiM against standard care. Twelve warships were randomized into treatment and control groups and were evaluated over the course of 12–18 months. The study found no evidence of the program's effectiveness but also no evidence of harm (Greenberg et al., 2010). The second study was a non-randomized parallel-group comparison trial that aimed to evaluate TRiM's effects on the posttrauma reactions of two personnel groups: one that was in the initial stages of using TRiM (TRiM-naïve) and a second that had adopted TRiM several years earlier and had incorporated it into the group's distinctive organizational culture (TRiM-experienced). The TRiM-experienced group reported lower levels of psychological distress than the TRiM-naïve group both pre- and post-deployment (Frappell-Cooke et al., 2010). While TRiM is a promising model, these studies fall short of providing convincing evidence of the positive impact of this intervention.

Few studies have examined the effectiveness of peer-support programs in improving resilience or reducing psychological health problems among law enforcement personnel or first responders, and there are even fewer methodologically rigorous studies. A study of peer-support programs for police officers in New York City found that officers were more willing to access mental health assistance with the encouragement of peers (New York University Center on Violence and Recovery, 2008). The study did not specifically address the effectiveness of the services received (Grauwiler, Barocas, and Mills, 2007). One recent publication assessed peer support as a way to reduce burnout among physicians, but that study was largely descriptive and did not provide convincing evidence of efficacy (Shapiro and Galowitz, 2016). A similar study conducted a few years earlier concluded that colleagues trained in peer support were the most commonly identified potential sources of support for physicians experiencing stress or trauma (Hu et al., 2012).

While there are many examples of peer-support interventions, there is considerable diversity in the structure and intended goals of these programs, and there have been few studies of the effectiveness of peer-support programs for increasing resilience and reducing psychological health problems among populations similar to the DHS workforce. The overall level of certainty of a net benefit of peer-support programs is low.

Approaches for Responding to Traumatic Incidents and High Levels of Workplace Stress

As described in Chapter Two, DHS employees often work under high levels of stress; some are exposed to traumatic events and, as a result, increased potential for injury or death in the line of duty. Several interventions have emerged to support psychological well-being after such traumatic events, and findings supporting such interventions have risen to the level of national attention. Five of the most prominent and widely used approaches for responding to psychological needs in the aftermath of a traumatic incident and other causes of heightened stress are (1) critical incident stress management (CISM), (2) critical incident stress debriefing (CISD), (3) psychological first aid (PFA), (4) stress first aid (SFA), and (5) mental health first aid (MHFA). These types of interventions are delivered shortly after the trauma and can range in duration. The goals of each are to reduce the psychological impact of trauma or stress and to minimize negative mental health outcomes among those exposed.

Critical Incident Stress Management

CISM is an umbrella term for a variety of programs that include debriefing sessions for acute crisis response, pre-incident preparedness, and post-crisis follow-up. CISM programs vary according to the type of critical incidents being addressed; the number, timing, and content of debriefing sessions; the individuals delivering the program; and whether the intervention is provided in an individual or group setting.

CISM was developed as an integrated system that includes pre-incident training, initial post-incident defusing, group debriefing, and further counseling if needed (Mitchell and Everly, 1997). The International Critical Incident Stress Foundation has defined the following seven core components of CISM:

1. pre-crisis preparation, which includes stress management education, stress resistance, and crisis mitigation training for both individuals and organizations
2. disaster or large-scale incident, school, and community support programs, including demobilizations, informational briefings, town-hall meetings, and staff advisement
3. defusing, a three-phase, structured, small-group discussion conducted within hours of a crisis for purposes of assessment, triaging, and acute symptom mitigation
4. CISD, a structured group discussion designed to mitigate acute symptoms, assess the need for follow-up, and if possible, provide a sense of post-crisis psychological closure
5. one-on-one crisis intervention/counseling or psychological support across the crisis spectrum
6. family crisis intervention and organizational consultation
7. follow-up and referral mechanisms for assessment and treatment, if necessary (adapted from Everly and Mitchell, undated).

Critical Incident Stress Debriefing

CISD, a component of CISM, has been used as for decades as a stand-alone intervention following traumatic events, though evidence for its effectiveness in preventing psychological health problems is mixed. While there is some variation in CISD (e.g., who administers it, whether it is administered in an individual or group setting), the intervention has two principal intentions: (1) to reduce levels of psychological distress after traumatic incidents and (2) to prevent the development of psychiatric disorders (e.g., PTSD, depression, substance use disorder). It originated in a military context as a way to maintain group morale and reduce psychiatric distress among personnel immediately after combat (Rose et al., 2002). It was adapted for civilians in the 1980s and spread widely among law enforcement and first responder communities (Dyregov, 1989). Debriefing has been used with a considerable range of populations, many with roles similar to those within DHS, such as police officers, members of the military, rescue workers involved in natural disaster response, and train operators who have witnessed someone die of suicide by train. Despite the intervention's widespread use, reviews of high-quality randomized and quasi-randomized trials concluded that single-session individual debriefing does not prevent PTSD (McNally, Bryant, and Ehlers, 2003; Rose et al., 2002). Individuals exposed to a trauma who received a debriefing intervention were just as likely to develop PTSD as individuals who received either no intervention or an educational intervention. In fact, at least two studies reported that debriefing was associated with an increased risk of PTSD (Bisson et al., 1997; Hobbs et al., 1996).

Although single-session individual debriefing is contraindicated, the evidence for group debriefing is less definitive. One randomized controlled trial of group CISD with emergency workers (67 volunteer firefighters) found that the intervention was associated with less alcohol use post-intervention and significantly greater post-intervention quality of life relative to the control group. It did not find significant effects on PTSD or psychological distress (Tuckey and Scott, 2014).

Evidence for CISM

Most research on the effectiveness of CISM has been in non–law enforcement settings (Müller-Leonhardt et al., 2014). A pragmatic comparative field trial compared the effectiveness of CISM as a whole with the effectiveness of stand-alone CISD in reducing symptoms of PTSD among victims of armed robbery. The structured CISM package of care demonstrated better outcomes than stand-alone CISD (Richards, 2001). A 2003 literature review on CISM focused on the implications of the intervention's use with emergency service personnel. The study concluded that CISM has no impact on preventing PTSD or other psychiatric symptoms following a traumatic event and found that some studies showed an increase in stress-related symptoms (Bledsoe, 2003).

It is important to note that many studies on CISM and CISD suffer from serious methodological shortcomings, including absent or inequivalent comparison groups, sampling bias, and small samples. Regardless, CISD is largely contraindicated for trauma response due to the risk of negative outcomes. The certainty of a net benefit of this practice is low, and it should no longer be recommended as a best practice. The evidence for CISM is less conclusive than for CISD. Given that much CISM research has been conducted with populations that do not generalize well to DHS employees, coupled with the frequent methodological flaws in the existing research, the certainty of a net benefit of CISM is also low.

Psychological, Stress, and Mental Health First Aid

Several alternatives to CISD exist and are being used to varying degrees with military, law enforcement, and first responder communities.

Psychological First Aid

PFA, designed by the National Child Traumatic Stress Network and the U.S. Department of Veterans Affairs (VA) National Center for PTSD, is an evidence-informed approach to reducing initial post-traumatic distress, as well as improving short- and long-term adaptive function, through a systematic set of helping actions. The VA/U.S. Department of Defense clinical practice guidelines for the management of PTSD recommend PFA for management of acute stress and discourage debriefing (Nash and Watson, 2012; Ruzek et al., 2007). A key feature of PFA is that it does not assume that everyone who experiences a traumatic event will suffer from mental health problems. Survivors may experience a wide variety of triggers and reactions that manifest through diverse symptoms with differing intensities. The PFA approach acknowledges these differences when treating survivors of traumatic or critical incidents (Brymer et al., 2006).

In 2010, the American Red Cross directed one of its subcommittees to review existing evidence on PFA from 1990 to 2010 with the goal of determining whether it is a "safe, effective and feasible intervention for first-aid providers without professional mental health training when confronted with people who have experienced a traumatic event" (Fox et al., 2012, p. 248). The review concluded that PFA was a vital first step to ensuring basic care, comfort, and support but that providers must be trained and reminded that PFA is intended to assist victims with their initial needs but not serve as a treatment. The review identified objective observational studies and a consensus of expert opinion to support the use of PFA. However, the authors characterized this literature as "evidence-informed" rather than "evidence-based," because it had not yet moved into the realm of truly analytic studies (e.g., randomized trials with strong methodologies) (Fox et al., 2012, p. 250). The level of certainty of a net benefit of PFA is moderate.

Stress First Aid

A similar but distinct intervention, SFA, was pioneered by the U.S. military through its Combat and Operational Stress First Aid (COSFA) program. The Navy, Marine Corps, Defense Centers of Excellence for Psychological Health and Traumatic Brain Injury, and VA National Center for PTSD collaborated to develop COSFA to replace CISD and provide a more effective stress management program to personnel (Nash, 2011). PFA was intended to be a public-facing intervention for primary survivors of disasters, whereas COSFA was developed specifically for peer support and self-care in high-risk occupations. COSFA maps onto five empirically supported elements of interventions that have been shown to be related to better recovery from a broad range of ongoing adverse events (Hobfoll et al., 2007): (1) promotion of a sense of safety, (2) promotion of calming, (3) promotion of sense of self and collective efficacy, (4) promotion of connectedness, and (5) promotion of hope. COSFA uses a stress-continuum model to inform decisions regarding when an intervention is needed, the type of intervention to provide, assessment of recovery, and indications for bridging to higher levels of care (Vashdi, Bamberger, and Bacharach, 2012; Nash and Watson, 2012).

Although COSFA has been widely implemented across the U.S. Department of Defense, there does not appear to be any evaluations of its effectiveness in increasing resilience or preventing psychological health problems. It has, however, since been adapted for use with fire and emergency medical service professionals, law enforcement personnel, medical personnel, and railway employees. The SFA model is meant to be used in situations of ongoing stress with employees and peers in high-risk occupations, rather than in post-disaster settings. Therefore, the SFA model may be a more appropriate fit for adapting to government employees who experience ongoing stress. Unfortunately, given the paucity of peer-reviewed evidence, the level of certainty of a net benefit of SFA is low. A randomized controlled trial is currently being conducted with fire and emergency medical service professionals, and, if it is methodologically sound, the approach could be an important contribution to this body of literature.

Mental Health First Aid

MHFA is a third related but distinct program designed to equip individuals to recognize the signs of mental illness and substance use disorders and to provide immediate support and assistance (Kitchener and Jorm, 2008). MHFA, which was originally developed in Australia, was launched in the United States in 2008. Since then, it has spread widely, and legislation in support of MHFA has been proposed in at least 23 states (National Council for Behavioral Health, 2014). A recent meta-analysis of the effectiveness of MHFA concluded that, overall, the evidence is reasonably strong that individuals trained in MHFA experience improvements in mental health knowledge, more favorable beliefs about treatment, increased help-provision behaviors, and reduced stigma. However, confidence in the effectiveness of MHFA is hampered by two significant limitations. First, the evidence of positive impact is limited to those already trained in MHFA, and there is no evidence of effectiveness among potential recipients (Wong, Collins, and Cerully, 2015). Second, the populations included in evaluations of MHFA effectiveness are not easily generalizable to the DHS workforce. Due to these limitations, the level of certainty of a net benefit of this intervention is moderate.

Conclusion

The evidence summarized in this chapter pertains to a selection of resilience-building and psychological disorder prevention approaches that are either relevant to existing DHS programs or common prevention interventions that could be applicable to the type of work done by DHS employees. Overall, there is limited evidence supporting these types of interventions due to a paucity of high-quality studies (Table 3.1). This may be a result of the newness of this field of research or the challenge presented by the relative infrequency of traumatic

Table 3.1
Summary of Findings on Workplace Approaches to Promoting Resilience and Preventing Psychological Health Problems

Intervention	Purpose	Certainty of Positive Net Impact Based on Available Evidence
EAPs	Strategic guidance, support, and consultation offered internally to an organization or through an external provider to assist with personal or family issues	Moderate
Short-term counseling	Brief, solution-focused counseling to address general conditions of living and issues specific to the individual, such as stress management, adjustment challenges (e.g., reassignment, geographical moves), interpersonal problems, financial or employment issues, and grief and loss	Low-moderate
Self-care	Activities to nurture the self and promote well-being, such as meditation, mindfulness practice, moderate exercise, journaling, taking deliberate breaks from work or home tasks, participating in meaningful activities, or limiting unnecessary exposure to trauma	Low
Resilience training	Intervention before a problem appears, including educational programming or training on risk, strategies to manage stress and other risk factors, and recognizing warning signs of a developing problem	Low overall but moderate for commercial training programs for civilian populations
Peer support	Peer-based intervention to help individuals respond to stress, including training for peer supporters to connect affected individuals with resources or to provide case management support, education, or counseling	Low
CISM	Acute crisis response, sometimes including pre-crisis and post-crisis components	Low
CISD	Structured, small-group acute crisis debriefing, either formal or informal, within 72 hours of event	Low; contraindicated
PFA	Response to individual psychological needs resulting from a disaster or traumatic event	Moderate
SFA	Response to individual psychological needs resulting from job-related stress or traumatic events	Low
MHFA	Response to individual needs of a person developing a mental health condition or having a mental health crisis	Moderate

events and ethical concerns related to conducting research on people who experience such events.

Based on our criteria for levels of certainty in the net benefit of approaches, none of the approaches examined here had sufficient evidence for high certainty. Only five approaches rose to the level of moderate certainty: (1) EAPs, (2) short-term counseling (for civilian populations only), (3) commercial resilience training programs (for civilian populations only), (4) PFA, and (5) MHFA. All others had a low certainty of net benefit. There are important caveats for some of these low-certainty approaches, however. Although the evidence is limited with regard to military populations for both resilience training and short-term counseling, the evidence from civilian populations is promising. In addition, the lack of evidence for the use of SFA is likely due to its relative newness compared with the other first aid–type approaches. It was designed using similar evidence and principles as PFA, and a randomized controlled trial of its effectiveness is under way.

CHAPTER FOUR

DHS Programs to Address Psychological Health

As described in Chapter Two, DHS employees may face work-related psychological health risks. Mitigating these risks and ensuring the availability of appropriate resources are critical tasks for OHA and component agencies. In this chapter, we describe the programs in place in seven components and across DHS aimed at reducing psychological health problems. For the purposes of this report, we defined a *program* as an organizational effort to provide a structured set of services, resources, or interventions that address psychological health among members of the DHS community. In the sections that follow, we describe programs provided by OHA and component EAPs that are available to employees across DHS. We then describe and compare programs available in selected DHS component agencies.

DHS Office of Health Affairs

In 2009, the Deputy Secretary of Homeland Security established a program within OHA to address the department's poor FEVS scores and perceptions of higher-than-average suicide rates among DHS employees. This program, DHS*Together*, was a DHS-wide employee and organizational resilience program with a mission "to enhance the health and well-being of all DHS employees" (DHS OHA, 2016b). The program provided resources to employees to build individual resilience and minimize suicide risk, and it provided support to component agencies, such as information and resources (e.g., posters, brochures), financial support to launch psychological health programs (e.g., peer support), and technical assistance (e.g., guidance for starting new programs). As part of this effort, in 2015, DHS*Together* launched an individual resilience assessment tool for employees, based on a validated resilience measure (Connor and Davidson, 2003). The goal of the tool was to provide employees with a baseline resilience score and personalized feedback on strategies to increase resilience (DHS OHA, 2016a). Employees were encouraged to continually monitor their resilience, but there was no method for monitoring whether they were pursuing the recommended actions.[1]

Beginning in 2015, DHS*Together* worked with several component agencies, including USCIS, USSS, U.S. Border Patrol, and the National Protection and Programs Directorate, to develop peer-support programs, including providing financial support (such as a limited amount of funding for training, materials, and staff) and technical assistance. Rather than implement a DHS-wide approach to peer support, DHS*Together* focused on working with individual components to establish peer-support programs tailored to the needs of the component. To facilitate information sharing, it established the Peer Support Community of Practice, a group of key peer-support contacts in each component.

In June 2016, the Assistant Secretary of Homeland Security for Health Affairs/Chief Medical Officer established the Behavioral Health Branch (BHB) within OHA; the mission of the BHB is "to provide tailored guidance to the Office of Health Affairs (OHA) leadership and DHS components on workforce psychological health issues."[2] DHS*Together* was subsumed as a program within BHB, and its name has since been discontinued. BHB focuses on improving the psychological health and well-being of the DHS workforce and has developed initiatives to address occupational stress, resilience, health promotion, crisis response, stigma reduction, and prevention of workplace violence and suicide.[3]

---

[1]   Interview with OHA staff, February 2017.

[2]   Interview with OHA staff, September 2017.

[3]   Interview with OHA staff, September 2017.

As a guiding principle for its initiatives, BHB uses an approach adapted from the U.S. Marine Corps Combat and Operational Stress Continuum Model (U.S. Marine Corps, 2010). The DHS Health and Performance Continuum Model (Figure 4.1) classifies health and functioning along a continuum from "optimal health" to "severe stress symptoms." According to BHB leadership, "This model integrates the following points: (1) psychological health and fitness is important to overall performance, (2) the involvement of medical and behavioral health personnel increases as a DHS employee moves to the right of a resilient state, and (3) recovery is encouraged and promoted at every point of the continuum."[4] BHB views the continuum as a way to "help to keep the DHS workforce ready and resilient, and well positioned to support our national security mission." To achieve this goal, BHB plans to use a variety of prevention and early intervention approaches, including mindfulness resilience training, sleep optimization/fatigue management, and a psychological health and resilience website.[5]

At the time of our study, BHB was planning to continue initiatives started by DHS*Together* specifically for "at-risk individuals and groups," such as peer support and psychological first aid, as well as advertising the treatment services available. To support component agencies in addressing workforce psychological health needs, BHB established the Resilience, Health and Performance Leadership Committee, composed of OHA behavioral health and human capital staff and DHS operational and training academy representatives. The purpose of the committee is "to establish component needs in the areas of resilience, psychological health, and performance; share best practices; facilitate collaboration; and [ensure the] scalability of future resilience initiatives that enhance the health and well-being of the DHS workforce."[6] BHB was also partnering with OCHCO to promote policies that promote good health and performance that are under that office's purview, such as employee engagement, morale, and the FEVS.

---

[4] Interview with OHA staff, September 2017.

[5] Interview with OHA staff, September 2017.

[6] Interview with OHA staff, September 2017.

Figure 4.1
OHA Health and Stress Continuum

◄ *Resilient*   *Stressed* ►

Peak health	Decreased health	Poor health	Impaired health
Optimal health	**Mild stress symptoms**	**Moderate stress symptoms**	**Severe stress symptoms**
• Good sleep • Focused attention • Sustained energy • Physically fit • Sense of humor • Optimistic • Socially connected • Self-confident • Hobbies • Meaningful work and relationships	• Mild sleep loss • Decreased attention • Reduced energy • Displaced sarcasm • Increased alcohol use • Excessive eating • Mild anxiety/ irritability • Decreased exercise • Social avoidance • Decreased work performance	• Nightmares • Difficulty focusing • Low energy • Frequent headaches • Weight gain • Alcohol misuse • Moderate anxiety/ sadness • Guilt • Social withdrawal • Procrastination • Absenteeism	• Sleep deprivation • Memory problems • Exhaustion • Somatic symptoms • Alcohol and drug abuse • PTSD • Depression/ hopelessness • Suicidal thoughts • Social isolation • Destructive or unethical behavior
Health-promotion activities (primary prevention)	**Stress-reduction activities (secondary prevention)**	**Stress-reduction activities (secondary prevention)**	**Clinical health services (tertiary prevention)**
• Regular exercise • Sleep optimization • Good diet/portion control • Problem-solving skills • Emotional-intelligence skills • Time with family and friends • Recreation/ volunteerism • Mindfulness/ yoga/martial arts	• Peer support and chaplain programs • EAP • Balanced diet/ portion control • Psychological first aid • Increased social activities • Regular exercise • Spiritual practice	• Peer support and chaplain programs • EAP • Good diet/portion control • Psychological first aid • Increased social engagement • Regular exercise • Spiritual practice	• Federal benefits/ private insurance • Evidence-based psychological and medication therapies • Dietitian consultation • Cognitive behavior therapy • Marital counseling • Physical trainer • Work reintegration plan

SOURCE: Provided by OHA.
NOTE: The continuum was in development at the time of our research.

Employee Assistance Programs

Each DHS component agency offers an EAP as a benefit to its employees. As noted in Chapter Three, there is moderate certainty that EAPs have a positive net impact on participants, according to available evidence. The services offered by component EAPs are fairly consistent across DHS (Table 4.2). All EAPs offer short-term counseling, though the number of counseling sessions per employee and the depth of the counseling varies by component. For example, some components offer a total of six sessions per year, while another offers six sessions per issue per year, and another offers unlimited short sessions. All the EAPs also provide access to a 24-hour phone line, though some direct employees to a national hotline or to the cell phones of on-call component staff instead of an EAP-run hotline. All DHS EAPs also offer some form of financial advice, services, or information to employees, as well as general health and wellness information and support for life challenges. Most have a web portal where employees can access resources and information about services, referrals, and wellness tips. In ICE, TSA, and USSS, EAP providers play a prominent role in critical incident response; in these components, EAP counselors are involved in a structured response (often also including peer support) from the onset of an incident. In other components, EAP providers play a supportive role in responding to critical or traumatic incidents only if requested by component staff or if an employee self-initiates counseling services. Finally, some EAPs offer coaching sessions or consultations to supervisors and managers.

With the exception of USSS, which has had its own EAP since 1984, components contract with an external vendor to provide EAP services. Most components employ an internal staff member who collaborates with the EAP contractor or assumes responsibility for the program's execution (e.g., ICE has a blended internal/external EAP). In our interviews, some component representatives noted challenges associated with external contractors, such as counselors who are not trained in the unique needs of DHS employees. General counselors available through external EAP providers may not be trained in DHS cultural competencies or be knowledgeable about specific job stressors.

Table 4.2
EAP Services, by DHS Component

Component	Short-term Counseling	Financial Services	Legal Services	Wellness/ Life Challenges	Online Resources	Critical Incident Response	Supervisor Consultations	24/7 Call Line
CBP	✓	✓		✓	✓			✓
FEMA	✓	✓	✓	✓	✓	✓	✓	✓
FLETC	✓	✓	✓	✓	✓		✓	✓
ICE	✓	✓	✓	✓	✓	✓	✓	✓
TSA	✓	✓	✓	✓	✓	✓	✓	✓
USCIS	✓	✓		✓	✓		✓	✓
USSS	✓	✓	✓	✓		✓	✓	✓

NOTE: This information is from a review of EAP websites and brochures and from interviews with component representatives. EAPs may offer additional resources and services that are not explicitly listed here.

This issue may be trivial in locations rich with therapeutic resources, such as urban areas, or if component staff provide training to EAP counselors. However, many DHS employees (particularly in CBP and FEMA) are stationed in rural or remote locations with limited access to appropriately trained counselors. This could be a reason that many components reported that EAP services were underutilized. Although internal EAPs could pose a challenge in terms of employees' perception of privacy and confidentiality (Walsh, 1982), they may be better able to customize services and counselor training specifically to meet DHS employee needs.

Psychological Health Programs Provided by DHS Component Agencies

To characterize the types of psychological health programs available across the DHS components in our study, we identified existing programs through our interviews and then categorized these programs according to the type of services they provided. We categorized the type of service provided based on the approaches for preventing or reducing psychological health problems described in Chapter Three: short-term counseling, self-care, resilience training, peer support, and traumatic/critical incident response. Table 4.3 provides an overview, by component, of the psychological health programs and services available to DHS employees as of February 2017. In the sections that follow, we describe these programs in more detail. The appendix includes a full list and more detailed descriptions of all the programs we identified.

Short-Term Counseling and Self-Care

As shown in Table 4.2 and discussed earlier, all DHS EAPs provide short-term counseling services in all component agencies. To augment this resource, ICE and CBP Air and Marine Operations (AMO) employ licensed mental health providers outside of the components' EAPs who are available to employees for counseling sessions. USCIS was in the process of hiring a physician with expertise in mental and behavioral

Table 4.3
Psychological Health Programs and Services, by DHS Component

Component	Peer Support	Traumatic/ Critical Incident Response	Short-Term Counseling	Self-Care	Resilience Training
CBP	Fully implemented	Provided through EAP via peer-support training	Fully implemented in a subcomponent/ division; provided through EAP	Provided through EAP	Fully implemented
FEMA	No programs available	Provided through EAP	Provided through EAP	Provided through EAP	
FLETC	Fully implemented	Provided through EAP via peer-support training	Provided through EAP	Fully implemented; provided through EAP	Fully implemented
ICE	Fully implemented	Provided through EAP via peer-support training	Fully implemented; provided through EAP	Provided through EAP	Fully implemented
TSA	Fully implemented in a subcomponent/ division	Fully implemented in a subcomponent/ division; provided through EAP	Provided through EAP	Provided through EAP	Pilot or in development
USCIS	Pilot or in development	Pilot or in development	Provided through EAP	Provided through EAP	Fully implemented
USSS	Pilot or in development	Provided through EAP via peer-support training	Provided through EAP	Provided through EAP	

SOURCE: Review of DHS program materials and interviews with OHA staff.

health at the time of our interview with staff from that component.[7] These mental health providers are available to employees for counseling sessions when needed, but they do not provide medical treatment for diagnosed mental health conditions. Based on the available evidence, there is low to moderate certainty that short-term counseling has a positive net impact on participants. EAPs also provide a variety of self-care tools to component employees. While employees themselves must be responsible for self-care, EAPs provide tools and resources to assist them. Although the specific tools provided by DHS EAPs have not been formally researched, self-care overall has a low certainty of a positive net impact.

Resilience Training

A number of component agencies have developed programs to increase the resilience of their employees. CBP provides resilience training to border patrol agents through its Border Patrol Academy curriculum. All trainees learn about peer support, chaplaincy, suicide prevention, and wellness and resilience during standard academy training. Some trainees attend a pre-academy training session; these trainees receive more in-depth training on these topics, as well as additional training in PFA with the goals of reducing line-of-duty deaths (through the Below 100 program), improving relationships and reducing stress (Strong Bonds program), and increasing awareness of how to best use available mental health resources. The full program was to be available to all trainees in the academy starting in the fourth quarter of 2017. At the time of this writing, CBP was in the process of establishing a structured resilience program to serve as an umbrella for all existing resilience training efforts (e.g., peer support, chaplaincy, suicide prevention, wellness).

ICE recently established a resilience programs unit that houses four psychological health programs: peer support, EAP, work-life balance, and chaplaincy. According to an interviewee, the unit's guiding principles for building resilience are to make employees feel that ICE

---

[7] Interview with USCIS staff, January 2017.

cares about them and for employees to be proud of their workplace.[8] FLETC and USCIS offer resilience training to employees on a variety of topics, including PTSD management, stress reduction, employee wellness (health and nutrition), meditation, and suicide prevention. As with self-care, the resilience programs used by DHS components have not been formally researched and evaluated, but the general certainty of a positive net impact of resilience training interventions is low to moderate.

Peer-Support Programs

As described earlier, peer support can take a number of forms. In the DHS context, OHA uses the term *peer support* to refer to a broad array of psychological health approaches, including gatekeeper training, critical incident response, and PFA. All peer-support programs in DHS components incorporate elements of these approaches, but the peer-support training curricula and terminology used to describe these elements varied across programs. While peer-support programs have a low certainty of a positive net impact based on the evidence provided in Chapter Three, PFA (included as a part of some DHS peer-support programs) has moderate certainty.

DHS peer supporters are employees who are selected to receive specific training in peer support and commit to spending a portion of their work time (often collateral duty) providing support to their fellow employees. Peer supporters in DHS generally provide one-on-one support, group support alongside a mental health provider, referrals to services, and critical or traumatic incident response. Peer supporters are often called upon for grief support following traumatic incidents and to assist with personal issues, such as family and relationship stressors.

FEMA is the only component we reviewed that did not offer a peer-support program. All other component agencies had fully implemented peer-support (CBP, FLETC, and ICE), had programs in the pilot or development phase (USCIS and USSS), or offered such a program in a subcomponent (TSA's Federal Air Marshal Service [FAMS]). To ensure adequate access to peer support, the number of peer sup-

---

8   Interview with ICE staff, December 2016.

porters in most component agencies is based on a ratio of peer supporters to the number of employees in the component. For example, we learned in our interviews that TSA's goal is to have one peer supporter for every 20 employees. CBP, the component with the largest number of employees, has the largest peer-support program, with 750 employees who have received training in peer support and 660 active peer supporters.

In most components, peer supporters are required to track their peer-support activities. While the type of information that peer supporters are required to report varies, most components require information on the number and type of contacts, as well as the type of support provided (see Table 4.4). This information is collected in a database that component program managers can monitor and could be used for evaluation purposes. While some components have conducted internal evaluations, no component peer-support program had been formally evaluated by an external organization at the time of our study.

Peer supporters undergo anywhere from two to ten days of training, with each component selecting or designing a curriculum that suits its needs (Table 4.5). Many components use a curriculum designed by the International Critical Incident Stress Foundation, Inc. (ICISF), while others incorporate elements from the International Association of Chiefs of Police or other sources. Most training covers the basics of peer support, critical incident response, suicide prevention, and PFA. Some components with longer training requirements (e.g., CBP, ICE) go into greater depth on these topics and address other issues, such as mood disorders, delivering death notifications, and cultural awareness and competency.

Across components, respondents noted some common barriers to employees' use of peer support. Several interviewees cited a lack of access to peer supporters as a critical barrier for certain employees. For example, some CBP (including AMO and the Office of Field Operations [OFO]) employees are located in remote or hard-to-access locations without peer supporters on site. Other interviewees reported that there were not enough peer supporters in general because training opportunities were infrequent. One interviewee noted that some supervisors restrict employees' time, making it difficult for employees

Table 4.4
Peer Support Programs, by DHS Component

Component	Division	Peer Supporters	Eligibility Requirements	Selection Process	Contact Database	Reporting Requirements	Information Collected
CBP	U.S. Border Patrol	Trained: 750 Active: 660 Goal: 850	3+ years of experience; approval from chain of command	Self-identify, approval from supervisor, and interview	Yes	Mandatory reporting monthly	• Type (topics/categories) of contact • Number of contact hours
CBP	AMO	Trained: 35 Active: 30 Goal: 60+	3+ years of experience; approval from chain of command	Self-identify, approval from supervisor, and interview	Yes	Mandatory reporting monthly	• Type (topics/categories) of contact • Time spent per contact
CBP	OFO	Trained: 400 Active: 400 Goal: 500	3+ years of experience	Self-identify, approval from supervisor, and interview	Yes	Mandatory reporting quarterly	• Type (topics/categories) of contact • Location of contacts • Type of support provided
FLETC	HQ	Trained: 100+ Active: 40 Goal: N/A	All FLETC and partner organization staff	Self-identify, approval from supervisor, interview, vetting, and unanimous vote by CISM staff	Yes	Mandatory reporting monthly	• Type (topics/categories) of contact • Staff or student contact • Date of contact • Time spent per contact • Type of referral provided

Table 4.4—Continued

Component	Division	Peer Supporters	Eligibility Requirements	Selection Process	Contact Database	Reporting Requirements	Information Collected
ICE	HQ	Trained: 350 Active: 315 Goal: 550	3+ years of experience, law enforcement experience, or helping profession experience (or combination)	Self-identify, approval from supervisor, submit memo of interest, and interview	Yes	Mandatory reporting monthly	• Type (topics/categories) of contact • Type of support provided
TSA	FAMS	Trained: 400 Active: 300 Goal: 1:20 peer supporter–employee ratio	3+ years of experience; most recent performance rating of at least "achieved expectations"	Nomination by supervisor	Yes	Not mandatory	• Date of contact • Directorate of contact • Contact type (employee, family) • Mode of contact (e.g., phone, email) • Duration of contact • Type (topics/categories) of contact • Warning signs exhibited • Type of support provided • Type of referral provided • Location of contact
USCIS	Southeast region	Trained: 20 Active: 20 Goal: 100	Unknown	Self-identify or nomination, vetting, and screening by mental health professional	Yes	Mandatory reporting monthly	• Type (topics/categories) of contact • Type of support provided

Table 4.4—Continued

Component	Division	Peer Supporters	Eligibility Requirements	Selection Process	Contact Database	Reporting Requirements	Information Collected
USSS	HQ	Trained: 29 Active: 0 (until policy finalized) Goal: 100–150	Full-time, non-probationary, no other collateral duty involvement, not involved in disciplinary or investigative process	Self-identify, written approval from supervisor, vetting, and interview	In development	Mandatory reporting monthly	• Type (topics/categories) of contact • Location of contact (region)

SOURCES: Interviews with component staff, December 2016–February 2017.

NOTE: HQ = headquarters.

Table 4.5
Peer-Support Program Training Requirements, by DHS Component

Component	Division	Days	Instructor	Exam Required	Certificate Received	Number of Trainings Offered Annually	Number of Supporters Trained Annually	Required Refresher Training
CBP	U.S. Border Patrol	8–9	TBD	Yes	Yes	At least 5	120	Mandatory annually; 3-day training
CBP	AMO	5	Team clinician	Yes	Yes	1	25–35	Mandatory annually; 3-day training
CBP	OFO	10	ICISF/CBP	No	Yes	4–5	96	Mandatory annually; 3-day training
FLETC	HQ	5	ICISF-trained CISM staff	No	Yes	Varies	Varies	Mandatory annually, plus quarterly additional training
ICE	HQ	9	Resilience program staff	Yes	Yes	4–6	96–144	Mandatory every two years
TSA	FAMS	2–3	ICISF staff	No	Yes	6–10	150–200	Not required
USCIS	Southeast region	5	Unknown	Yes	Yes	Unknown	Unknown	Mandatory every two years
USSS	HQ	3	Private contractor: mental health clinicians	Yes	Yes	1–2	N/A	Mandatory annually; 3-day training

SOURCES: Interviews with component staff, December 2016–February 2017.
NOTE: HQ = headquarters.

to seek support while on the job. Because some programs were still new, not all employees (and family members, if applicable) were aware of how to access peer supporters or even of programs' existence. Some peer-support managers reported that employees did not use peer support out of concern about stigma around seeking help or fears that their employment status or job description would suffer if a supervisor found out they needed support. For example, interviewees noted that some USSS and CBP employees were concerned that their clearance or gun would be revoked after confiding in a peer (see also DHS, 2013).

While most DHS peer-support programs focus on serving employees, some extend services to family members or other members of the community (see the appendix). For example, peer-support programs in FLETC and TSA FAMS provide peer-support services in the case of a traumatic incident to employees' family members or to employees of affiliated organizations, such as local law enforcement personnel. Funding for peer-support programs differs somewhat by component. Established peer-support programs in CBP, FLETC, ICE, and TSA FAMS have incorporated program funding (ranging from $100,000 to $1 million) into their annual budgets. Newer programs, such as those in USSS and USCIS, have received financial support from OHA to start the program, with the expectation that these components will also self-fund peer support once the programs are established.

In our interviews, many component peer-support program managers reported that they anticipated changes to their programs. CBP was updating its peer-supporter training and preparing to merge its OFO and AMO programs into one unified CBP peer-support training program. CBP was looking into changing its database to better track the number of employees served. Both FLETC and ICE were making staffing adjustments. FLETC was planning to add additional program support staff, and ICE was onboarding two new full-time peer-support managers. ICE's peer-support program was establishing health and wellness working groups for employees who experience trauma. These groups, facilitated by peer supporters, would offer physical, psychological, social, and spiritual support to employees. USCIS was moving to expand its pilot peer-support program in its southeast region to all of USCIS.

Critical or Traumatic Incident Response

In most component agencies, critical or traumatic incident response is a function of peer-support programs combined with the services of EAP licensed mental health care providers. The approach to critical or traumatic incident response is very similar across components. When an incident occurs (e.g., line-of-duty death, suicide, shooting), a dedicated staff member (e.g., peer-support program manager or other leadership) coordinates with key staff, including the local peer-support manager or someone at the location where the incident occurred, to develop a plan of action. Typically, the incident response plan includes deploying local peer supporters and a component or EAP licensed mental health care provider to the office of the employee(s) involved in the incident. In most components, this response process is automatically implemented as soon as the incident has occurred. In USSS, a supervisor must first contact the EAP before a response effort is launched.

In some cases, peer supporters from outside the local area will be brought in if the event is deemed too traumatic for local peer supporters (e.g., if the peer supporters will need support themselves), if a particular peer supporter has relevant expertise, or if there are not enough (or any) peer supporters at the incident location. At the time of our interviews, ICE was planning to deploy a chaplain and a human resource professional (a family liaison with training in peer support) for all incidents in which benefits would need to be activated, such as in the case of serious injury or death. For extremely traumatic incidents, CBP would deploy a coordinated team of peer supporters from all divisions (Border Patrol, AMO, and OFO).

Once the traumatic incident response team arrives at the incident site, the team meets with affected employees both one on one and in groups. Activities include group informational briefings about the incident, group debriefings, individual counseling and support, and referral to services. Most component interviewees reported using CISM techniques recommended by the ICISF (Everly and Mitchell, undated), which includes CISD. USSS has made it mandatory to offer affected employees a debriefing about the incident, though employees can decline. As noted previously, both CISM and CISD have a low certainty of positive net impact, and CISD specifically is contraindicated, as there is evidence of a negative net impact on participants.

Across components, peer supporters play a supportive role in traumatic incident response. They do not provide counseling or conduct debriefings, as these are conducted by licensed mental health care providers. CBP peer supporters also assist families in a logistical capacity if there is a death or serious injury by helping with transportation (e.g., driving people to the hospital, picking up family members from the airport). Peer supporters across all programs stay at the incident site for varying lengths of time.

Other Programs and Related Initiatives in Development

Two components (CBP and FLETC) use chaplains as a psychological health resource for employees and their families; at the time of this writing, ICE was also in the process of establishing a chaplaincy program. Chaplaincy programs perform many of the same functions as peer-support programs, including providing one-on-one support, critical incident response, and referrals. Chaplains may serve in additional roles in the event of a line-of-duty death, including performing ceremonial functions. Chaplains must undergo training similar to peer-support training, and some chaplains (e.g., CBP OFO) are required to log their contacts in a component database. OFO employees reportedly use chaplains more often than peer supporters; CBP OFO chaplains serve 86,000 people annually, including in ceremonial roles.

Outside of structured programs, most components offer additional training, seminars, events, or resources related to psychological health. Several offer training on available resources during employee orientation, including peer support and EAPs. Throughout the year, many offer optional online and in-person training on specific subjects, such as suicide prevention and alcohol risk awareness. Some components have made selected training mandatory, though it is not common. Some component representatives also described occasional seminars with guest speakers or other special events, such as health fairs. These initiatives are typically sporadic and voluntary for employees.

At the time of this research, USSS was in the process of developing a program for employees in the Violent Crimes Against Children division. This program, known as Safeguard, would aim to foster wellness and mitigate risks to employees exposed to crimes against children by conducting trainings and providing educational materials. In addition, USSS was planning to develop a work-life balance program for employees. USCIS was in the process of establishing a critical incident group to address violence in the workplace. This program would provide training to supervisors and resources to other employees on how to handle violent situations at work. More details about these programs are available in the appendix.

Conclusion

DHS has a number of existing psychological health programs managed at the headquarters level by OHA and programs developed and managed by individual components. All components, with the exception of FEMA, have implemented a peer-support program either component-wide or within a division. However, the nature of these programs and the type of training that peer supporters receive differ significantly across components. Many components rely on their EAP to provide short-term counseling to employees, while others have hired a dedicated mental health provider to supplement the services offered by the component EAP. In our interviews, many component representatives described plans for programs that were in development; we note that our description of existing programs was current as of February 2017 and may change over time.

Of the programs identified across DHS, four program types have a moderate or low-moderate certainty of a positive net impact (EAPs, short-term counseling, resilience training, and PFA). Of all the interventions described in this report, the only intervention we reviewed that had moderate certainty and was not found in any DHS program was MHFA, though this intervention may have limited utility in the DHS context compared with similar first-aid approaches. Despite the low certainty of a positive net impact of many current DHS programs (e.g., peer support), it is important to note that research is limited or lacks rigor for many interventions. Additional research to assess the effect of these programs on DHS workforce well-being, resilience, and other outcomes is essential.

CHAPTER FIVE

Summary and Recommendations

In previous chapters, we described major stressors that DHS employees may face, presented the evidence on workplace psychological health interventions, and described the psychological health programs available DHS-wide and in selected DHS components. In this chapter, we discuss the limitations of our findings and provide recommendations for improving programs and services across DHS. The recommendations are based on our interviews with OHA and other DHS component representatives and our review of the research on workplace psychological health interventions. Because each DHS component has a different mission, the services and care that employees need will also differ. Therefore, our recommendations should be adapted to the unique needs of each component and for DHS as a whole.

Limitations

It is important to note that this assessment has some limitations that should be considered when interpreting the findings. First, while we conducted a robust review of the literature, we did not aim to conduct a systematic literature review or meta-analysis. It is possible that we overlooked some studies examining the effectiveness of the approaches to preventing mental health problems and increasing resilience that we describe in this report. We think it is unlikely, however, that we missed any studies that would have changed our conclusions about the level of evidence for these interventions.

Second, we conducted interviews with a limited number of personnel in OHA and in each component. OHA provided us with a list of contacts—generally one person per component agency. In most cases, these contacts were program managers or other individuals with primary responsibility for psychological health programs in the component. Through these original contacts, we identified a small number of additional interviewees. However, it was not possible to conduct interviews with personnel in every component location that might have housed a relevant program (e.g., TSA programs in each airport); as a result, our study may have omitted some locally administered programs. We did not interview DHS employees or others who had participated in or were aware of the programs, such as law enforcement personnel or union representatives. We also did not interview DHS or component leadership, who may have had different perspectives on the function, purpose, and future of psychological health programs.

Third, component interviewees provided information about the programs discussed in this report, including the content and characteristics of each program; we were not able to independently verify this information. Although our interviewees had the opportunity to review our description of their component or program, not all interviewees responded to confirm the accuracy of the information.

Fourth, this report identifies programs to improve resilience and reduce psychological health problems among DHS employees. As we noted in Chapter Two, organizational culture plays a significant role in employee well-being. While DHS may be taking steps to improve organizational culture, this study did not attempt to describe such efforts. We note that the American Psychological Association's Center for Organizational Excellence (undated) has developed a set of five workplace practices (employee engagement, work-life balance, employee growth and development, health and safety, and employee recognition) that could be considered as a model for such an organization-wide effort. We suggest that future studies assess the appropriateness of these or similar approaches for the DHS context.

Finally, the programs described in this report represent a snapshot as of February 2017, and the context for the BHB was updated in September 2017. Programs are constantly evolving, ending, or being added, and it is possible that programs began or ended after we concluded our data collection. Notably, we conducted this assessment shortly after the 2016 election. With any change in presidential administration, the missions of Cabinet-level departments or component agencies may also change, as could the scope, relevance, or priority of psychological health programs in DHS.

Recommendations

Drawing on our review of the research literature and interviews with DHS program managers and subject-matter experts, we offer several recommendations to improve the availability of psychological health programs across DHS and to ensure that existing programs are following best practices.

Recommendation 1. Ensure That All DHS Employees Have Access to Psychological Health Support

DHS employees consistently report lower morale and engagement than other federal employees (GAO, 2012; Maurer, 2013), and many have occupations and roles that are inherently stressful. To improve resilience and morale and to prevent psychological health problems, DHS should ensure that all employees can access adequate support. However, the evidence base for most approaches to building resilience and preventing psychological health problems is fairly weak. The majority of research on these types of interventions is descriptive in nature, employs a flawed analytic methodology (e.g., small sample size, no randomization, a poorly matched control group or none at all), or fails to show a significant relationship between interventions and desired outcomes. The evidence for preventing future psychological health problems is particularly thin. This may be due, in part, to the complexity of psychological health conditions and the difficultly of showing a causal relationship between a single event or ongoing stressor and later development of such a condition. Despite these limitations, there is stronger support for some of the approaches outlined in Chapter Three than for others.

In our review of existing psychological health programs across DHS, we found that most operational components had a variety of programs and resources for employees, including peer-support programs and resiliency training. Some of these programs were in development or in pilot phases and had not been rolled out across the entire component. The exception was FEMA: According to our interviews with OHA and component representatives, there were no programs in place (aside from an EAP) to support the psychological health of FEMA employees at the time of our research. Given that FEMA employees and temporary staff—particularly those deployed after a disaster—may face unique stressors and have a higher risk of work-related stress, secondary trauma, and psychological health problems, we recommend that DHS assess the need for psychological health support for these employees (see Recommendation 4.1) and consider implementing programs analogous to those available in other operational components.

Recommendation 1.1. Consider Providing Access to a DHS-Trained Licensed Mental Health Care Provider in Each Operational Component

Short-term counseling has been shown to improve certain indicators of workplace well-being, such as the amount of sick leave taken and self-reported workplace motivation (McLeod, 2010). The evidence supporting its use for mitigating psychological health problems is somewhat less convincing, but most studies did show either a positive or null impact. All the DHS component representatives we interviewed reported that their components made short-term counseling available through their EAP. CBP, FLETC, ICE, TSA, and USSS had licensed mental health care providers on their staffs, separate from the component's EAP, to provide varying degrees of support to employees. We recommend that all DHS components consider providing access to a licensed mental health care provider—specifically trained in the stressors and needs of component employees—to provide targeted, short-term counseling. To accomplish this, components could train EAP providers in DHS and component-specific cultural competencies or hire an internal mental health care provider. Components with employees in disparate locations might consider making a mental health care provider available on-site in the location with the most employees, but, ideally, they would also provide dedicated hours for remote employees to call the provider and a travel stipend for the provider to visit other component locations throughout the year.

Recommendation 2. Ensure That There Are Clear Policies for Peer-Support Programs in All Operational Components

Peer support has been a main focus for improving the psychological health of employees. CBP, FLETC, ICE, TSA, USCIS, and USSS have already established peer-support programs either component-wide or for a subset of employees. As peer-support programs expand to all components, we recommend establishing clear and consistent policies to help ensure their success.

Peer support has a well-documented impact on psychological well-being in specific populations, particularly the severely mentally ill, but it is not possible to generalize these findings to the DHS workforce. While peer-support programs have been implemented widely among populations that are similar to DHS employees, such as military personnel, law enforcement officers, and physicians, the evidence to support their effectiveness in improving psychological health is still quite limited, and the level of certainty of a positive net impact is low. Given that best practices for peer-support programs have not yet been established, we recommend that DHS consider mechanisms to increase the effectiveness of these programs and minimize unintended harms.

Recommendation 2.1. Develop Formal Policies for All Peer-Support Programs

Policies on peer-support programs should outline all duties that peer supporters can and cannot perform, what training is required for performing those duties, what peer supporters can and cannot be held accountable for in their role, the resources in place to assist peer supporters, and the management plan and chain of command for peer supporters within the component. When such a policy is shared with all staff, those who use peer-support services will also understand the roles and responsibilities of peer supporters within the larger context of the component. To establish such a policy or to incorporate this guidance into existing policies, peer-support managers and component leadership must collaboratively determine what resources peer supporters need to successfully fulfill their role (e.g., access to counselors, regular and standardized training). They also must determine and clearly articulate the boundaries of the peer-support role and how it fits within other component policies and systems.

Recommendation 2.2. Ensure That Peer Supporters Receive Effective Training, Including Refresher Training at Regular Intervals

As described in Chapter Four, the type, duration, and intensity of training that peer supporters receive varies across components. We recommend that OHA develop a standardized peer-supporter training and certification program, based on the best available evidence, that includes training in SFA/PFA (see Recommendation 3). While each component may wish to tailor the training to meet its specific needs or to reflect component-specific situations, the basic elements of the training should not vary across DHS. OHA should also develop a model for refresher training and set standards for its frequency.

Recommendation 3. Replace Formal Debriefing with a First-Aid Model

Employees may use the term *debriefing* to describe informal conversations within their peer group after a stressful event or during stressful periods. These types of informal, unstructured conversations should not be discouraged if employees are willing participants. Formal debriefing—discussed in this report as CISD but sometimes known by other names, such as *psychological debriefing*—is a structured, short-term, small-group crisis response intervention. While this approach is widely accepted in law enforcement and emergency services populations, the evidence does not support its continued use. As discussed in Chapter Three, the literature shows that debriefing does not result in a lower risk of PTSD among individuals exposed to trauma. Furthermore, there is evidence that debriefing has a negative effect on resilience and vulnerability to PTSD.

We found that many components (CBP, FLETC, TSA, and USSS) practice debriefing in some form. CBP, FLETC, and TSA reported using the ICISF's CISM model, which includes psychological debriefing as a component of critical incident response. USSS's EAP conducts debriefings with employees involved in critical incidents, who can accept or decline services. DHS could increase the resilience of its workforce by replacing debriefing with SFA or PFA for those who experience a high-trauma event or who work in a high-stress role. SFA was initially developed as a replacement for CISD in military contexts and has since been adopted by other professions. Because this approach is newer than the other first-aid interventions discussed in this report, the evidence base is limited, resulting in a low certainty of a positive net impact. However, the SFA model maps closely to evidence-informed principles that are relevant in continuous stress situations like those faced by many DHS employees. PFA, designed for those who survive a disaster or experience a traumatic event, may be less relevant for DHS, but it is supported by expert opinion and has been found to be effective in limited evaluations.

PFA or SFA would make a suitable replacement for debriefing in these types of programs because they are designed to be used in the same context as debriefing but are better supported by evidence. MHFA, which has a moderate certainty of positive net impact, may be considered as a replacement in certain circumstances, though it is designed to respond to mental health conditions and crises more specifically. Effective use of SFA/PFA requires consistent training of both professionals and peers, practicing skills between traumatic events, and ongoing training as SFA/PFA procedures are further developed. The National Fallen Firefighters Foundation is the main provider of SFA training through courses delivered either in person or online. PFA training using different PFA models is provided by a wide range of organizations, including the Red Cross, the National Center for PTSD, the National Child Traumatic Stress Network, VA, Coursera, and the John Hopkins School of Public Health. DHS would likely need to tailor any SFA/PFA training to its own needs, but these existing programs could serve as useful models. Beyond implementing this training for new programs, effective implementation of SFA/PFA will require retraining any currently engaged peer supporters and EAP providers, as well as ensuring that future training across DHS uses SFA or PFA approaches.

Recommendation 4. Optimize Management of Psychological Health Programs Across DHS

DHS is a large, complex organization, and, as we have discussed in this report, there have been numerous efforts across the department to address the psychological health of employees. To ensure that these efforts are coordinated and to optimize the management of its portfolio of programs, DHS should develop mechanisms for ensuring consistency across psychological health programs and components.

Recommendation 4.1. Conduct a Psychological Health Needs Assessment Prior to Developing New Programs

In Chapter Two, we described the psychological health risks and needs of DHS employees and noted that they vary considerably by occupation type and component. There has been little research on these risks, and there are few assessments of the prevalence of psychological health problems among DHS employees. This may be because such analyses are quite difficult. One approach to bridge this gap would be to examine the frequency of mental health disorder diagnoses recorded in health care claims data. This approach is used frequently in analyses of military psychological health problems. However, while the Office of Personnel and Management maintains a repository of health claims data for all federal employees, these data have not typically been available for research. An alternative would be to conduct a survey of all DHS employees that includes questions about work-related stress and screening items to detect potential psychological health problems. If such items could be added to an annual required survey, the cost and effort to obtain those data would be minimal relative to fielding a new survey.

Given the challenges associated with these approaches, a more reasonable alternative may be to conduct a qualitative assessment with subgroups of employees thought to be at highest risk, selected according to job type or component. In such an assessment, structured interviews and focus groups with employees and managers, followed by content analysis, could yield important information about the psychological health problems faced by these groups. The findings could be used to inform decisions about the nature and availability of future psychological health programs. In the absence of a formal needs assessment, reviewing the data from existing peer-support and chaplain databases could provide a cursory overview of the most pressing issues among those who seek services.

Recommendation 4.2. Develop Clear Definitions for Psychological Health Program Types Across DHS

Due to the decentralized nature of DHS, each component has autonomy in establishing its own programs and defining the conceptual models associated with each program. While flexibility is important, the lack of consistent definitions can make categorizing and comparing programs in each component a challenge. In particular, the term *peer support* often means different things in different contexts. In some contexts, peer support could be understood as informal conversation between peers, while formal peer support is a more intensive mental health intervention. Centrally developing clear definitions for the types of psychological health programs offered across DHS could increase efficiency and effectiveness across the department. In addition, DHS should establish a clear delineation between peer support and other, more-intensive interventions.

Components incorporate many psychological health programs into their peer-support training. Categorizing other types of preventive or treatment approaches, such as resiliency training or SFA/PFA, within peer support could result in confusion among program managers and beneficiaries. For instance, many DHS employees transfer between components (e.g., between CBP and ICE) and, in the process, they may misunderstand what services are available to them in their new role, which may be detrimental at a time when services are most needed. Furthermore, without clear definitions of psychological health services, employees working in different divisions within a component may inadvertently design programs with duplicative or conflicting definitions. Finally, there is no system to accurately and comprehensively identify and track programs across components, making comparisons and accurate assessments of effectiveness challenging. Adopting a centralized conceptual framework and definitions of psychological health programs and services across DHS could address these barriers.

Recommendation 4.3. Monitor Psychological Health Programs Across DHS on an Ongoing Basis

This report provides a snapshot of programs in selected DHS components as of February 2017. Inevitably, this list of programs will change over time as funding, priorities, and staffing change within components. DHS should develop a mechanism for maintaining a list of all psychological health programs across the department. Ideally, this inventory should include all programs in every location, including those in local offices. Maintaining an up-to-date inventory of all programs may help DHS improve efficiency and ensure that resources and information are being distributed to all affiliated contacts and programs.

Recommendation 4.4. Establish Collaborative Networks Among Psychological Health Programs, Component Leadership, and Headquarters Leadership

We identified many psychological health programs and initiatives across DHS; while there may be informal efforts to coordinate across these programs, there is an opportunity for better communication about best practices, challenges, and lessons learned across existing programs and component and headquarters leadership. DHS should consider mechanisms to increase collaboration across the department. One option would be to build on the existing Resilience, Health and Performance Leadership Committee and establish a collaborative network of psychological health program managers, component leadership, and OHA/BHB staff. Regular meetings could identify both organizational and clinically oriented strategies for addressing psychological health issues in the workplace and serve as an opportunity to discuss ongoing programs (see Recommendation 5). For example, collaborative network meetings could be an ideal time to review the quarterly data from the peer-support databases across components (see Recommendation 5.2). This recommendation aligns with the DHS Office of the Inspector General report's vision for "unity of effort" to put structural changes in place to streamline and coordinate efforts across components (Roth, 2016). Using a collaborative approach to psychological health could help components learn from one another and increase ownership and responsibility for employee well-being, psychological health, and job satisfaction across DHS.

Recommendation 5. Build Evaluation into Psychological Health Programs

Evaluations provide a systematic mechanism for identifying what works in programs through defined methods for collecting, analyzing, and using data. Results from evaluations can be used to develop centralized resources, improve implementation strategies, adapt programs for different settings, and improve overall effectiveness. Without a systematic process for evaluation, untested programs could inadvertently result in harm to those who participate in them. None of the programs identified in this study have had a formal evaluation by an external organization, and DHS has evaluated only six programs in two components. In a 2016 report, the DHS Office of the Inspector General highlighted the need for program evaluation and performance measurement as a critical government business practice for DHS (Roth, 2016). Evaluation may be especially helpful in raising the certainty of many of the programs with a low level of certainty of a positive net impact.

We acknowledge that there are both policy and financial implications in incorporating evaluation into psychological health programs across the department. We recommend that DHS weigh the value of program evaluation relative to increasing support for ongoing or new programs. Program evaluation does not need to be expensive and can be built into ongoing program management activities, as described next. In considering the costs associated with evaluation, it is important to understand that evaluation and performance management can increase the efficacy of ongoing programs and thus ensure the most effective use of limited resources.

Recommendation 5.1. Develop Criteria to Assess Program Effectiveness

All DHS psychological health programs, especially those receiving funding from OHA, should embed ongoing evaluation into their efforts. However, before an evaluation is possible, the goals of these programs must be clear and agreed-upon. OHA, component leadership, program managers, or other stakeholders may have different goals for these programs. For example, one set of stakeholders may consider the goal of a particular psychological health program to be improved FEVS scores, while another set may consider the goal to be increased resilience among the workforce. Any evaluation needs to start with a clear focus on the intended outcomes of the program, how those outcomes will be measured (e.g., how do you define *success*?), and available data to measure outcomes. Given the long list of potential outcomes for DHS psychological health programs, we recommend selecting a few specific, measurable outcomes to measure and monitor over time.

Recommendation 5.2. Encourage Consistent Data Collection Across Component Programs

To conduct evaluations, programs must collect data that can be used to assess effectiveness. Many programs currently collect data on peer-support program use—for example, requiring peer supporters to report the nature of each contact and whether referrals were provided. We recommend that every program establish such a database and that the information collected be consistent across components. To ensure higher-quality data, reporting should be mandatory and regular (e.g., semiweekly). Peer supporters are unlikely to recall each of their contacts if they are required to report them less frequently. In addition, as mentioned, each program should consider collecting data on its outcomes to enable an assessment of whether it is meeting its goals. The data collected should not include any personally identifiable information to ensure the confidentiality of the employees who use the program's services.

Recommendation 5.3. Encourage Programs to Implement Quality Improvement Processes

After identifying program goals and collecting relevant data on outcomes, program managers should assess whether the program is accomplishing its intended goals. If not, program managers should determine where problems are arising, identify and implement potential solutions, and continually monitor outcomes to ensure that the program meets its goals (Ryan et al., 2014). By focusing on quality improvement, DHS components' can begin to incorporate evaluation into their existing psychological health programs.

There are a variety of established methods for incorporating program evaluation and quality improvement into ongoing programs. The following are three examples:

- The Crisis Counseling Assistance and Training Program developed by the Substance Abuse and Mental Health Services Administration was designed to provide short-term assistance to disaster survivors. The toolkit provides guidance on how to measure what the agency defines as the three critical performance areas: program reach, quality, and consistency (Substance Abuse and Mental Health Services Administration, 2018).
- Getting To Outcomes (GTO) was developed at RAND to help communities plan, implement, evaluate, improve, and sustain prevention programs (RAND Corporation, undated). The ten steps of the GTO model aim to ensure program success; the first steps involve planning activities, followed by process and outcome evaluations, and then data analysis to improve programs. GTO helps communities and program managers incorporate lessons learned into existing operations.
- *A Program Manager's Guide for Program Improvement and Ongoing Psychological Health and Traumatic Brain Injury Programs* is a tool developed by RAND to assist those responsible for implementing or managing programs in the U.S. Department of Defense (Ryan et al., 2014). The tool was designed specifically for government settings and accounts for the fact that the individual managing the program may not have been responsible for creating it or have

control over its implementation. The tool may be relevant for DHS, as it focuses on program improvement overall, rather than addressing specific elements of programs that could vary from component to component.

Recommendation 5.4. Consider External Evaluations of Large or Critical Programs

We recommend that DHS consider having an external organization conduct a formal evaluation of some programs to ensure objectivity in reporting. DHS might select programs for external evaluation that are large, in terms of either the number of employees served or cost, or those that are deemed critical to the department's mission. Those responsible for programs may inherently report on them in an overly positive manner or omit negative findings; an external evaluation would provide an unbiased, objective assessment of the program's effectiveness.

Final Thoughts

DHS employees are the front line for ensuring the safety and security of the United States. These jobs are inherently stressful and can involve exposure to emotional or traumatic events for some employees. Organizational culture also plays a significant role in employee well-being. Workplace stress contributes to worse job performance, burnout, and other negative outcomes; addressing and improving the psychological health of employees can yield benefits for the department as a whole. DHS has consistently ranked among the lowest achievers in the FEVS. Improving employee well-being, and raising FEVS scores, was named a top priority by former Secretary of Homeland Security John Kelly. This is not a new priority, however; raising this ranking has long been a chief concern of DHS and led to the creation of DHS*Together* and, subsequently, BHB, which has focused on optimizing DHS workforce health and resilience.

To improve DHS employees' psychological well-being, the department must address their specific psychological health needs and concerns and measure the effectiveness of existing programs that address psychological health. Our study suggests that the evidence base for most psychological health interventions is relatively weak. While a peer-support program and other resilience initiatives may add nominal value and improve employee well-being overall, ensuring that these programs are both effective and beneficial to employees is paramount. The recommendations in this report provide a way forward for building on the momentum already under way. Establishing a centralized evidence base by building evaluation into all programs will help DHS determine whether the investments being made in these programs are achieving their desired outcomes for DHS, its employees, and their families.

Psychological Health Programs, by Component, in the U.S. Department of Homeland Security

Table A.1 lists the psychological health programs offered by each DHS component and their status at the time this research was conducted in November 2017.

Table A.1
Psychological Health Programs in DHS

Component and Subcomponent	Program Type	Stage of Development	Program Description	Date Established	Written Policy	Mandatory or Optional	Participants	Number Served Annually	Evaluation Conducted
CBP									
U.S. Border Patrol	Peer support	Fully implemented	Provide peer support to CBP staff and support following critical or traumatic events	1999 (regionally); 2006 (nationally)	Yes	Optional	Employees, trainees, and families	27,457 contact hours[a]	Internal only
HQ	Critical/traumatic incident response	Early-stage launch	Activate Border Patrol, AMO, and OFO peer support to large-scale traumatic events	2010	No	Optional but highly recommended	Employees, trainees, and families	N/A	No
AMO	Peer support	Fully implemented	Primarily, provide critical incident response; peer support is secondary	2008	Yes	Optional	Employees and families	~300–600	No
OFO	Peer support	Fully implemented	Provide peer support to OFO staff and provide support following critical or traumatic events	2012	Yes	Optional	Employees and families	~1,100	Internal only
	Chaplain program	Fully implemented	Provide spiritual support to OFO employees	2011	Yes	Optional	Employees and families	~86,000	Internal only
U.S. Border Patrol Academy	Resiliency program	Fully implemented	Educate trainees about peer support, chaplaincy, suicide prevention, and wellness and resiliency	2016	No	Mandatory	Trainees and families	Total in academy (~300–400)	No

Table A.1—Continued

Component and Subcomponent	Program Type	Stage of Development	Program Description	Date Established	Written Policy	Mandatory or Optional	Participants	Number Served Annually	Evaluation Conducted
FEMA									
HQ	No programs available	N/A	N/A	N/A	N/A	N/A	N/A	N/A	N/A
FLETCs									
HQ	Peer support	Fully implemented	Provide brief, solution-focused stress management and individual crisis intervention	1999	Yes	Optional	Employees, partner org staff, students, and families	~460	Internal only
	Critical/ traumatic incident response	Fully implemented	Provide clinical and peer support following a critical or traumatic event	2006	Yes	Optional	Employees, partner org staff, students, and families	~400–460	Internal only
	Chaplain program	Fully implemented	Provide spiritual support when requested through peer support program	2006	In peer support policy	Optional	Employees, partner org staff, students, and families	In peer support program total	Internal only

Table A.1—Continued

Component and Subcomponent	Program Type	Stage of Development	Program Description	Date Established	Written Policy	Mandatory or Optional	Participants	Number Served Annually	Evaluation Conducted
ICE									
HQ	Peer support	Fully implemented	Provide peer support on a limited basis to address personal issues, and provide critical support following critical or traumatic events	2013	Yes	Optional	Employees and families	1,098 in FY 2016	No
	Chaplain program	Information gathering	Provide spiritual support	Planned for FY 2018	In process	Optional	Employees and families	N/A	N/A
	Critical/ traumatic incident response	Fully implemented	Provide clinician and peer support following a critical or traumatic event	2013	Yes	Optional	Employees and families	881 in FY 2016	No
TSA									
HQ	No programs available	N/A	N/A	N/A	N/A	N/A	N/A	N/A	N/A
FAMS	Critical/ traumatic incident response	Fully implemented	Provide clinician and peer support following a critical or traumatic event	2010	Yes	Optional	Employees, families, and local police	~850	No

Table A.1—Continued

Component and Subcomponent	Program Type	Stage of Development	Program Description	Date Established	Written Policy	Mandatory or Optional	Participants	Number Served Annually[a]	Evaluation Conducted
USCIS									
Southeast region	Peer support	Pilot	Provide peer support to employees in the Southeast region	2016	No	Optional	Employees	Unknown	No
HQ	Resiliency	Information gathering	Violence in the Workplace Critical Incident Group will assist employees experiencing domestic violence or violence in the workplace	Target was FY 2017	In process	Optional	Likely supervisors for training, all employees for resources	N/A	N/A
USSS									
HQ	Peer support	Pilot	Provide peer support to USSS staff and support following critical or traumatic events	Target was FY 2017	In process	Optional	Employees	N/A	No
	Critical/traumatic incident response	Fully implemented	Provide clinician and peer support following a critical or traumatic event	Unknown	Yes	Mandatory to offer (employees can decline)	Employees	N/A	No
	Resiliency	Information gathering	Safeguard Program will foster wellness and mitigate risks to employees	2017	No	Mandatory	Employees in Crimes Against Children	N/A	No

NOTE: HQ = headquarters. FY = fiscal year.
[a] Number of individuals served not available.

References

Adams, Richard E., Charles R. Figley, and Joseph A. Boscarino, "The Compassion Fatigue Scale: Its Use with Social Workers Following Urban Disaster," *Research on Social Work Practice*, Vol. 18, No. 3, 2008, pp. 238–250.

Agaibi, Christine E., and John P. Wilson, "Trauma, PTSD, and Resilience: A Review of the Literature," *Trauma, Violence, and Abuse*, Vol. 6, No. 3, July 2005, pp. 195–216.

American Psychological Association, "The Road to Resilience," webpage, undated. As of February 13, 2018:
http://www.apa.org/helpcenter/road-resilience.aspx

American Psychological Association, Center for Organizational Excellence, "Resources for Employers," webpage, undated. As of February 13, 2018:
https://www.apaexcellence.org/resources/creatingahealthyworkplace

Arnetz, Bengt B., Eamonn Arble, Lena Backman, Adam Lynch, and Ake Lublin, "Assessment of a Prevention Program for Work-Related Stress Among Urban Police Officers," *International Archives of Occupational and Environmental Health*, Vol. 86, No. 1, 2013, pp. 79–88.

Awa, Wendy L., Martina Plaumann, and Ulla Walter, "Burnout Prevention: A Review of Intervention Programs," *Patient Education and Counseling*, Vol. 78, No. 2, February 2010, pp. 184–190.

Baird, Katie, and Amanda C. Kracen, "Vicarious Traumatization and Secondary Traumatic Stress: A Research Synthesis," *Counselling Psychology Quarterly*, Vol. 19, No. 2, 2006, pp. 181–188.

Bakker, Arnold B., and Patrícia L. Costa, "Chronic Job Burnout and Daily Functioning: A Theoretical Analysis," *Burnout Research*, Vol. 1, No. 3, December 2014, pp. 112–119.

Benedek, David M., Carol Fullerton, and Robert J. Ursano, "First Responders: Mental Health Consequences of Natural and Human-Made Disasters for Public Health and Public Safety Workers," *Annual Review of Public Health*, Vol. 28, 2007, pp. 55–68.

Bennett, Joel B., Jeremy W. Bray, Daniel Hughes, Joan F. Hunter, Jodi Jacobson Frey, Paul M. Roman, and David A. Sharar, *Bridging Public Health with Workplace Behavioral Health Services: A Framework for Future Research and a Stakeholder Call to Action*, Employee Assistance Professionals Association, Employee Assistance Research Foundation, and Employee Assistance Society of America, September 2015. As of February 13, 2018:
http://archive.hshsl.umaryland.edu/bitstream/10713/4876/1/Bridging%20 Public%20Health%20.pdf

Berry, Leonard L., Ann M. Mirabito, and William B. Baun, "What's the Hard Return on Employee Wellness Programs?" *Harvard Business Review*, Vol. 88, No. 12, December 2010, pp. 104–112.

Bisson, Jonathan I., Peter L. Jenkins, Julie Alexander, and Carol Bannister, "Randomised Controlled Trial of Psychological Debriefing for Victims of Acute Burn Trauma," *British Journal of Psychiatry*, Vol. 171, No. 1, 1997, pp. 78–81.

Bledsoe, Bryan E., "Critical Incident Stress Management (CISM): Benefit or Risk for Emergency Services?" *Prehospital Emergency Care*, Vol. 7, No. 2, 2003, pp. 272–279.

Bowen, Gary L., "A Measure of Comprehensive Airman Fitness: Construct Validation and Invariance Across Air Force Service Components," *Military Behavioral Health*, Vol. 4, No. 2, 2016, pp. 149–158.

Brymer, Melissa, Christopher Layne, Anne Jacobs, Robert Pynoos, Josef Ruzek, Alan Steinberg, Eric Vernberg, and Patricia Watson, *Psychological First Aid Field Operations Guide*, National Child Traumatic Stress Network, 2006.

CBP—*See* U.S. Customs and Border Protection.

Chopko, Brian A., Patrick A. Palmieri, and Richard E. Adams, "Associations Between Police Stress and Alcohol Use: Implications for Practice," *Journal of Loss and Trauma*, Vol. 18, No. 5, 2013, pp. 482–497.

———, "Posttraumatic Growth in Relation to the Frequency and Severity of Traumatic Experiences Among Police Officers in Small to Midsize Departments," *Journal of Interpersonal Violence*, May 18, 2016.

Colwell, Lori H., Phillip M. Lyons, A. Jerry Bruce, Randall L. Garner, and Rowland S. Miller, "Police Officers' Cognitive Appraisals for Traumatic Events: Implications for Treatment and Training," *Applied Psychology in Criminal Justice*, Vol. 7, No. 2, 2011, pp. 106–132.

Connor, Kathryn M., and Jonathan R. T. Davidson, "Development of a New Resilience Scale: The Connor-Davidson Resilience Scale (CD-RISC)," *Depression and Anxiety*, Vol. 18, No. 2, 2003, pp. 76–82.

Connor, Kathryn M., Jonathan R. T. Davidson, and Li-Ching Lee, "Spirituality, Resilience, and Anger in Survivors of Violent Trauma: A Community Survey," *Journal of Traumatic Stress*, Vol. 16, No. 5, 2003, pp. 487–494.

Defense Manpower Data Center, *2010 Military Family Life Project (MFLP): Tabulations of Response*, Arlington, Va., ADA609601, 2011.

DHS—*See* U.S. Department of Homeland Security.

DHS OHA—*See* U.S. Department of Homeland Security, Office of Health Affairs.

Druss, Benjamin G., Liping Zhao, Silke A. von Esenwein, Joseph R. Bona, Larry Fricks, Sherry Jenkins-Tucker, Evelina Sterling, Ralph DiClemente, and Kate Lorig, "The Health and Recovery Peer (Harp) Program: A Peer-Led Intervention to Improve Medical Self-Management for Persons with Serious Mental Illness," *Schizophrenia Research*, Vol. 118, Nos. 1–3, May 2010, pp. 264–270.

Dyregov, Atle, "Caring for Helpers in Disaster Situations: Psychological Debriefing," *Disaster Management*, Vol. 2, No. 1, 1989, pp. 25–30.

Ekins, Emily E., *Policing in America: Understanding Public Attitudes Toward the Police. Results from a National Survey*, Washington, D.C.: Cato Institute, 2016.

Ellrich, K., and D. Baier, "Post-Traumatic Stress Symptoms in Police Officers Following Violent Assaults: A Study on General and Police-Specific Risk and Protective Factors," *Journal of Interpersonal Violence*, Vol. 32, No. 3, February 2017, pp. 331–356.

Elwood, Lisa S., Juliette Mott, Jeffrey M. Lohr, and Tara E. Galovski, "Secondary Trauma Symptoms in Clinicians: A Critical Review of the Construct, Specificity, and Implications for Trauma-Focused Treatment," *Clinical Psychology Review*, Vol. 31, No. 1, 2011, pp. 25–36.

Employee Assistance Trade Association, "What Is EAP?" webpage, undated. As of February 13, 2018:
https://www.easna.org/research-and-best-practices/what-is-eap

Everly, George, and Jeffrey Mitchell, *A Primer on Critical Incident Stress Management (CISM)*, International Critical Incident Stress Foundation, undated. As of February 13, 2018:
https://www.icisf.org/a-primer-on-critical-incident-stress-management-cism

Federal Emergency Management Agency, "FEMA's Mission Statement," webpage, last updated May 10, 2017. As of February 13, 2018:
https://www.fema.gov/media-library/assets/videos/80684

Federal Law Enforcement Training Centers, "Learn About FLETC," webpage, undated. As of February 13, 2018:
https://www.fletc.gov/learn-about-fletc

FEMA—*See* Federal Emergency Management Agency.

Figley, Charles R., "Compassion Fatigue: Psychotherapists' Chronic Lack of Self Care," *Journal of Clinical Psychology*, Vol. 58, No. 11, November 2002, pp. 1433–1441.

Flaxman, Paul E., and Frank W. Bond, "A Randomised Worksite Comparison of Acceptance and Commitment Therapy and Stress Inoculation Training," *Behaviour Research and Therapy*, Vol. 48, No. 8, 2010, pp. 816–820.

FLETC—*See* Federal Law Enforcement Training Centers.

Fox, Jeffrey H., Frederick M. Burkle, Judith Bass, Francesco A. Pia, Jonathan L. Epstein, and David Markenson, "The Effectiveness of Psychological First Aid as a Disaster Intervention Tool: Research Analysis of Peer-Reviewed Literature from 1990–2010," *Disaster Medicine and Public Health Preparedness*, Vol. 6, No. 3, 2012, pp. 247–252.

Frappell-Cooke, W., M. Gulina, K. Green, J. Hacker Hughes, and N. Greenberg, "Does Trauma Risk Management Reduce Psychological Distress in Deployed Troops?" *Occupational Medicine*, Vol. 60, No. 8, December 2010, pp. 645–650.

GAO—*See* U.S. Government Accountability Office.

Garbarino, S., N. Magnavita, M. Elovainio, T. Heponiemi, F. Ciprani, G. Cuomo, and A. Bergamaschi, "Police Job Strain During Routine Activities and a Major Event," *Occupational Medicine*, Vol. 61, No. 6, September 2011, pp. 395–399.

Gershon, Robyn R. M., Briana Barocas, Allison N. Canton, Xianbin Li, and David Vlahov, "Mental, Physical, and Behavioral Outcomes Associated with Perceived Work Stress in Police Officers," *Criminal Justice and Behavior*, Vol. 36, No. 3, 2009, pp. 275–289.

Gonzalez, Gabriella C., Reema Singh, Terry Schell, and Robin M. Weinick, *An Evaluation of the Implementation and Perceived Utility of the Airman Resilience Training Program*, Santa Monica, Calif.: RAND Corporation, RR-655-OSD, 2014. As of February 13, 2018:
https://www.rand.org/pubs/research_reports/RR655.html

Grafton, Eileen, Brigid Gillespie, and Saras Henderson, "Resilience: The Power Within," *Oncology Nursing Forum*, Vol. 37, No. 6, 2010, p. 698.

Grauwiler, Peggy, Briana Barocas, and Linda G. Mills, "Police Peer Support Programs: Current Knowledge and Practice," *International Journal of Emergency Mental Health*, Vol. 10, No. 1, 2007, pp. 27–38.

Greenberg, N., V. Langston, B. Everitt, A. Iversen, N. T. Fear, N. Jones, and S. Wessely, "A Cluster Randomized Controlled Trial to Determine the Efficacy of Trauma Risk Management (TRiM) in a Military Population," *Journal of Trauma Stress*, Vol. 23, No. 4, August 2010, pp. 430–436.

Harms, Peter D., Mitchel Herian, Dina V. Krasikova, Adam J. Vanhove, and Paul B. Lester, *The Comprehensive Soldier and Family Fitness Program Evaluation. Report #4: Evaluation of Resilience Training and Mental and Behavioral Health Outcomes*, Lincoln, Neb.: University of Nebraska, April 2013.

Hassed, Craig, Steven De Lisle, Gavin Sullivan, and Ciaran Pier, "Enhancing the Health of Medical Students: Outcomes of an Integrated Mindfulness and Lifestyle Program," *Advances in Health Sciences Education*, Vol. 14, No. 3, August 2009, pp. 387–398.

Hobbs, Michael, Richard Mayou, Beverly Harrison, and Peter Worlock, "A Randomised Controlled Trial of Psychological Debriefing for Victims of Road Traffic Accidents," *British Medical Journal*, Vol. 313, No. 7070, 1996, pp. 1438–1439.

Hobfoll, Stevan E., Patricia Watson, Carl C. Bell, Richard A. Bryant, Melissa J. Brymer, Matthew J. Friedman, Merle Friedman, Berthold P. R. Gersons, Joop T.V.M de Jong, Christopher M. Layne, Shira Maguen, Yuval Neria, Ann E. Norwood, Robert S. Pynoos, Dori Reissman, Josef I. Ruzek, Arieh Y. Shalev, Zahava Solomon, Alan M. Steinberg, and Robert J. Ursano "Five Essential Elements of Immediate and Mid-Term Mass Trauma Intervention: Empirical Evidence," *Psychiatry: Interpersonal and Biological Processes*, Vol. 70, No. 4, 2007, pp. 283–315.

Hu, Yue-Yung, Megan L. Fix, Nathanael D. Hevelone, Stuart R. Lipsitz, Caprice C. Greenberg, Joel S. Weissman, and Jo Shapiro, "Physicians' Needs in Coping with Emotional Stressors: The Case for Peer Support," *Archives of Surgery*, Vol. 147, No. 3, 2012, pp. 212–217.

ICE—*See* U.S. Immigration and Customs Enforcement.

Institute of Medicine, *A Ready and Resilient Workforce for the Department of Homeland Security: Protecting America's Front Line*, Washington, D.C.: National Academies Press, 2013.

IOM—*See* Institute of Medicine.

Kitchener, Betty A., and Anthony F. Jorm, "Mental Health First Aid: An International Programme for Early Intervention," *Early Intervention in Psychiatry*, Vol. 2, No. 1, 2008, pp. 55–61.

Korre, Maria, Andrea Farioli, Vasileia Varvarigou, Sho Sato, and Stefanos N. Kales, "A Survey of Stress Levels and Time Spent Across Law Enforcement Duties: Police Chief and Officer Agreement," *Policing*, Vol. 8, No. 2, 2014, pp. 109–122.

Kureczka, Arthur W., "Critical Incident Stress in Law Enforcement," *FBI Law Enforcement Bulletin*, Vol. 65, Nos. 2–3, 1996, pp. 10–16.

Leder, Johannes, Jan Alexander Häusser, and Andreas Mojzisch, "Exploring the Underpinnings of Impaired Strategic Decision-Making under Stress," *Journal of Economic Psychology*, Vol. 49, 2015, pp. 133–140.

Lerner, Debra, Angie Mae Rodday, Joshua T. Cohen, and William H. Rogers, "A Systematic Review of the Evidence Concerning the Economic Impact of Employee-Focused Health Promotion and Wellness Programs," *Journal of Occupational and Environmental Medicine*, Vol. 55, No. 2, 2013, pp. 209–222.

Loeppke, Ronald R., "Health and Productivity as a Business Strategy: A Multiemployer Study," *Journal of Occupational and Environmental Medicine*, Vol. 51, No. 4, 2009, pp. 411–428.

Mache, Stefanie, Monika Bernberg, Lisa Baresi, and David A. Groneberg, "Evaluation of Self-Care Skills Training and Solution-Focused Counselling for Health Professionals in Psychiatric Medicine: A Pilot Study," *International Journal of Psychiatry in Clinical Practice*, Vol. 20, No. 4, 2016, pp. 239–244.

Maddi, Salvatore R., Richard H. Harvey, Deborah M. Khoshaba, Mostafa Fazel, and Nephthys Resurreccion, "Hardiness Training Facilitates Performance in College," *Journal of Positive Psychology*, Vol. 4, No. 6, 2009, pp. 566–577.

Matos, Kenneth, and Ellen Galinsky, *2014 National Study of Employees*, New York: Families and Work Institute, 2014. As of February 13, 2018: http://familiesandwork.org/downloads/2014NationalStudyOfEmployers.pdf

Maurer, David C., Director of Homeland Security and Justice Issues, U.S. Government Accountability Office, *Department of Homeland Security: DHS's Efforts to Improve Employee Morale and Fill Senior Leadership Vacancies*, testimony before the Committee on Homeland Security, U.S. House of Representatives, Washington, D.C., GAO-14-228T, December 2013. As of February 13, 2018: http://www.gao.gov/assets/660/659642.pdf

Maxson, Cheryl, Karen Hennigan, and David C. Sloane, *Factors That Influence Public Opinion of the Police*, Washington, D.C.: U.S. Department of Justice, Office of Justice Programs, June 2003. As of February 18, 2018: https://www.ncjrs.gov/pdffiles1/nij/197925.pdf

McLeod, John, "The Effectiveness of Workplace Counselling: A Systematic Review," *Counselling and Psychotherapy Research*, Vol. 10, No. 4, 2010, pp. 238–248.

McNally, Richard J., Richard A. Bryant, and Anke Ehlers, "Does Early Psychological Intervention Promote Recovery from Posttraumatic Stress?" *Psychological Science in the Public Interest*, Vol. 4, No. 2, 2003, pp. 45–79.

Meadows, Sarah O., Laura L. Miller, and Sean Robson, *Airman and Family Resilience: Lessons from the Scientific Literature*, Santa Monica, Calif.: RAND Corporation, RR-106-AF, 2015. As of February 13, 2018: https://www.rand.org/pubs/research_reports/RR106.html

Meffert, Susan M., Clare Henn-Haase, Thomas J. Metzler, Meng Qian, Suzanne Best, Ayelet Hirschfeld, Shannon McCaslin, Sabra Inslicht, Thomas C. Neylan, and Charles R. Marmar, "Prospective Study of Police Officer Spouse/Partners: A New Pathway to Secondary Trauma and Relationship Violence?" *PLOS One*, Vol. 9, No. 7, 2014, article e100663.

Meredith, Lisa S., Cathy D. Sherbourne, Sarah J. Gaillot, Lydia Hansell, Hans V. Ritschard, Andrew Parker, and Glenda Wrenn, *Promoting Psychological Resilience in the U.S. Military*, Santa Monica, Calif.: RAND Corporation, MG-996-OSD, 2011. As of February 13, 2018:
http://www.rand.org/pubs/monographs/MG996.html

Mitchell, J. T., and G. S. Everly, "The Scientific Evidence for Critical Incident Stress Management," *Journal of Emergency Medical Service*, Vol. 22, No. 1, January 1997, pp. 86–93.

Morgado, P., N. Sousa, and J. J. Cerqueira, "The Impact of Stress in Decision Making in the Context of Uncertainty," *Journal of Neuroscience Research*, Vol. 93, No. 6, June 2015, pp. 839–847.

Morin, Rich, Kim Parker, Renee Stepler, and Andrew Mercer, "Behind the Badge," Pew Research Center, January 11, 2017. As of February 13, 2018:
http://www.pewsocialtrends.org/2017/01/11/behind-the-badge

Müller-Leonhardt, Alice, Shannon G. Mitchell, Joachim Vogt, and Tim Schürmann, "Critical Incident Stress Management (CISM) in Complex Systems: Cultural Adaptation and Safety Impacts in Healthcare," *Accident Analysis and Prevention*, Vol. 68, July 2014, pp. 172–180.

Nash, William P., "U.S. Marine Corps and Navy Combat and Operational Stress Continuum Model: A Tool for Leaders," *Combat and Operational Behavioral Health*, 2011, pp. 193–214.

Nash, William P., and Patricia J. Watson, "Review of VA/DOD Clinical Practice Guideline on Management of Acute Stress and Interventions to Prevent Posttraumatic Stress Disorder," *Journal of Rehabilitation Research and Development*, Vol. 49, No. 5, 2012, pp. 637–648.

National Council for Behavioral Health, *2014 Mental Health First Aid State Policy Toolkit*, 2014. As of February 13, 2018:
https://www.thenationalcouncil.org/wp-content/uploads/2014/08/Policy-Toolkit-FINAL.pdf

New York University Center on Violence and Recovery, "NYPD Peer Support Programs 3-Year Study Provides Groundbreaking Research," New York, April 16, 2008. As of February 13, 2018:
https://www.nyu.edu/about/news-publications/news/2008/april/nypd_peer_support_programs_3.html

Orem, Dorothea E., *Nursing: Concepts of Practice*, 4th ed., St. Louis, Mo.: Mosby Year Book, 1991.

Palm, Kathleen M., Melissa A. Polusny, and Victoria M. Follette, "Vicarious Traumatization: Potential Hazards and Interventions for Disaster and Trauma Workers," *Prehospital and Disaster Medicine*, Vol. 19, No. 1, January–March 2004, pp. 73–78.

Powell, Martine, Peter Cassematis, Mairi Benson, Stephen Smallbone, and Richard Wortley, "Police Officers' Strategies for Coping with the Stress of Investigating Internet Child Exploitation," *Traumatology: An International Journal*, Vol. 20, No. 1, 2014, pp. 32–42.

Pullen, Carol H., Patricia Hageman, Linda Boeckner, Susan N. Walker, and Maureen K. Oberdorfer, "Feasibility of Internet-Delivered Weight Loss Interventions Among Rural Women Ages 50–69," *Journal of Geriatric Physical Therapy*, Vol. 31, No. 3, 2008, pp. 105–112.

Radey, Melissa, and Charles R. Figley, "The Social Psychology of Compassion," *Clinical Social Work Journal*, Vol. 35, No. 3, 2007, pp. 207–214.

RAND Corporation, "Getting To Outcomes®: Improving Community-Based Prevention," webpage, undated. As of February 13, 2018: https://www.rand.org/health/projects/getting-to-outcomes.html

Repper, Julie, and Tim Carter, "A Review of the Literature on Peer Support in Mental Health Services," *Journal of Mental Health*, Vol. 20, No. 4, 2011, pp. 392–411.

Richards, David, "A Field Study of Critical Incident Stress Debriefing Versus Critical Incident Stress Management," *Journal of Mental Health*, Vol. 10, No. 3, 2001, pp. 351–362.

Robertson, Ivan T., Cary L. Cooper, Mustafa Sarkar, and Thomas Curran, "Resilience Training in the Workplace from 2003 to 2014: A Systemic Review," *Journal of Occupational and Organizational Psychology*, Vol. 88, No. 3, September 2015, pp. 533–562.

Robson, Sean, *Psychological Fitness and Resilience: A Review of Relevant Constructs, Measures, and Links to Well-Being*, Santa Monica, Calif.: RAND Corporation, RR-102-AF, 2014. As of February 13, 2018: https://www.rand.org/pubs/research_reports/RR102.html

Rose, Suzanna C., Jonathan Bisson, Rachel Churchill, and Simon Wessely, "Psychological Debriefing for Preventing Post Traumatic Stress Disorder (PTSD)," *Cochrane Database of Systematic Reviews*, April 22, 2002.

Roth, John, *Major Management and Performance Challenges Facing the Department of Homeland Security*, Washington, D.C.: U.S. Department of Homeland Security, Office of the Inspector General, OIG-17-08, November 2016.

Ruzek, Josef I., Melissa J. Brymer, Anne K. Jacobs, Christopher M. Layne, Eric M. Vernberg, and Patricia J. Watson, "Psychological First Aid," *Journal of Mental Health Counseling*, Vol. 29, No. 1, 2007, pp. 17–49.

Ryan, Gery W., Carrie M. Farmer, David M. Adamson, and Robin M. Weinick, *A Program Manager's Guide for Program Improvement in Ongoing Psychological Health and Traumatic Brain Injury Programs: The RAND Toolkit,* Vol. 4, Santa Monica, Calif.: RAND Corporation, RR-487/4-OSD, 2014. As of February 13, 2018: http://www.rand.org/pubs/research_reports/RR487z4.html

Salston, MaryDale, and Charles R. Figley, "Secondary Traumatic Stress Effects of Working with Survivors of Criminal Victimization," *Journal of Traumatic Stress,* Vol. 16, No. 2, April 2003, pp. 167–174.

Shapiro, Jo, and Pamela Galowitz, "Peer Support for Clinicians: A Programmatic Approach," *Academic Medicine,* Vol. 91, No. 9, 2016, pp. 1200–1204.

Sharar, David A., John C. Pompe, and Mark Attridge, "Onsite Versus Offsite EAPs: A Comparison of Workplace Outcomes," *Journal of Employee Assistance,* Vol. 43, No. 2, 2013.

Shoji, Kotaro, Magdalena Lesnierowska, Ewelina Smoktunowicz, Judith Bock, Aleksandra Luszczynska, Charles C. Benight, and Roman Cieslak, "What Comes First, Job Burnout or Secondary Traumatic Stress? Findings from Two Longitudinal Studies from the U.S. and Poland," *PLOS One,* Vol. 10, No. 8, 2015, article e0136730.

Sifaki-Pistolla, Dimitra, Vasiliki Eirini Chatzea, Sofia-Aikaterini Vlachaki, Evangelos Melidoniotis, and Georgia Pistolla, "Who Is Going to Rescue the Rescuers? Post-Traumatic Stress Disorder Among Rescue Workers Operating in Greece During the European Refugee Crisis," *Social Psychiatry and Psychiatric Epidemiology,* Vol. 52, No. 1, January 2017, pp. 45–54.

Steenkamp, Maria M., William P. Nash, and Brett T. Litz, "Post-Traumatic Stress Disorder: Review of the Comprehensive Soldier Fitness Program," *American Journal of Preventive Medicine,* Vol. 44, No. 5, May 2013, pp. 507–512.

Stice, Eric, Paul Rohde, Shelley Durant, Heather Shaw, and Emily Wade, "Effectiveness of Peer-Led Dissonance-Based Eating Disorder Prevention Groups: Results from Two Randomized Pilot Trials," *Behaviour Research and Therapy,* Vol. 51, Nos. 4–5, May 2013, pp. 197–206.

Substance Abuse and Mental Health Services Administration, "Evaluate Your CCP," webpage, last updated January 11, 2018. As of February 13, 2018: https://www.samhsa.gov/dtac/ccp-toolkit/evaluate-your-ccp

Thormar, Sigridur Bjork, Berthold Paul Rudolf Gersons, Barbara Juen, Adelheid Marschang, Maria Nelden Djakababa, and Miranda Olff, "The Mental Health Impact of Volunteering in a Disaster Setting: A Review," *Journal of Nervous and Mental Disease,* Vol. 198, No. 8, 2010, pp. 529–538.

Transportation Security Administration, "Mission," webpage, undated. As of February 13, 2018: https://www.tsa.gov/about/tsa-mission

TSA—*See* Transportation Security Administration.

Tuckey, Michelle R., and Jill E. Scott, "Group Critical Incident Stress Debriefing with Emergency Services Personnel: A Randomized Controlled Trial," *Anxiety, Stress, and Coping*, Vol. 27, No. 1, 2014, pp. 38–54.

USCIS—*See* U.S. Citizenship and Immigration Services.

U.S. Citizenship and Immigration Services, "About Us," webpage, last updated January 17, 2018. As of February 13, 2018:
https://www.uscis.gov/aboutus

U.S. Customs and Border Protection, "About CBP," webpage, last updated November 21, 2016. As of February 13, 2018:
https://www.cbp.gov/about

U.S. Department of Defense, *Annual Report to the Congressional Defense Committees on Plans for the Department of Defense for the Support of Military Family Readiness*, Washington, D.C., 2012.

U.S. Department of Homeland Security, "Peer Support Program: An Overview of the United States Border Patrol Peer Support Program," briefing slides, 2013. As of February 13, 2018:
http://nationalacademies.org/hmd/~/media/Files/Activity%20Files/HealthServices/DHSWorkforceResilience/2013-FEB-04/Presentation/Garrett%20ScottPSP%20IOM%20brief%2020130201.pdf

———, "Our Mission," web page, last updated May 11, 2016. As of February 13, 2018:
https://www.dhs.gov/our-mission

———, "Department Organizational Chart," April 12, 2017. Current organizational chart, as of February 13, 2018:
https://www.dhs.gov/organizational-chart

U.S. Department of Homeland Security, Office of Health Affairs, "Resilience Tool Fact Sheet," Washington, D.C, 2016a.

———, "Stress Management and Suicide Prevention Training," Washington, D.C. 2016b.

U.S. Government Accountability Office, *Department of Homeland Security: Taking Further Action to Better Determine Causes of Morale Problems Would Assist in Targeting Action Plans*, Washington, D.C., GAO-12-940, September 2012. As of February 13, 2018:
http://www.gao.gov/assets/650/648997.pdf

U.S. Immigration and Customs Enforcement, "Who We Are," webpage, last updated September 26, 2017. As of February 13, 2018:
https://www.ice.gov/about

U.S. Marine Corps, *Combat and Operational Stress Control*, Marine Corps Reference Publication 6-11C/Navy Tactical Techniques and Procedures 1-15M, 2010.

USPSTF—*See* U.S. Preventive Services Task Force.

U.S. Preventive Services Task Force, "Grade Definitions," webpage, last updated February 2013. As of February 13, 2018:
https://www.uspreventiveservicestaskforce.org/Page/Name/grade-definitions

U.S. Secret Service, "The Investigative Mission," webpage, undated(a). As of February 13, 2018:
https://www.secretservice.gov/investigation

———, "The Protective Mission," webpage, undated(b). As of February 13, 2018:
https://www.secretservice.gov/protection

USSS—*See* U.S. Secret Service.

Vashdi, D. R., P. A. Bamberger, and S. Bacharach, "Effects of Job Control and Situational Severity on the Timing of Help-Seeking," *Journal of Occupational Health Psychology*, Vol. 17, No. 2, April 2012, pp. 206–219.

Waite, Phillip J., and Glenn E. Richardson, "Determining the Efficacy of Resiliency Training in the Work Site," *Journal of Allied Health*, Vol. 33, No. 3, 2004, pp. 178–183.

Walsh, Diana Chapman, "Employee Assistance Programs," *Milbank Memorial Fund Quarterly: Health and Society*, Vol. 60, No. 3, 1982, pp. 492–517.

Warner, Kenneth E., Marc Meisnere, and Laura Aiuppa Denning, *Preventing Psychological Disorders in Service Members and Their Families: An Assessment of Programs*, Washington, D.C.: National Academies Press, 2014.

Webel, Allison R., Jennifer Okonsky, Joyce Trompeta, and William L. Holzemer, "A Systematic Review of the Effectiveness of Peer-Based Interventions on Health-Related Behaviors in Adults," *American Journal of Public Health*, Vol. 100, No. 2, 2010, pp. 247–253.

Wee, David F., and Diane Myers, "Stress Responses of Mental Health Workers Following Disaster: The Oklahoma City Bombing," in Charles R. Figly, ed., *Treating Compassion Fatigue*, New York: Brunner-Routledge, 2002, pp. 57–83.

Weinick, Robin M., Ellen Burke Beckjord, Carrie M. Farmer, Laurie T. Martin, Emily M. Gillen, Joie Acosta, Michael P. Fisher, Jeffrey Garnett, Gabriella C. Gonzalez, Todd Helmus, Lisa H. Jaycox, Kerry Reynolds, Nicholas Salcedo, and Deborah M. Scharf, *Programs Addressing Psychological Health and Traumatic Brain Injury Among U.S. Military Servicemembers and Their Families*, Santa Monica, Calif.: RAND Corporation, TR-950-OSD, 2011. As of February 13, 2018:
http://www.rand.org/pubs/technical_reports/TR950.html

Williams, Redford B., and Virginia P. Williams, "Adaptation and Implementation of an Evidence-Based Behavioral Medicine Program in Diverse Global Settings: The Williams LifeSkills Experience," *Translational Behavioral Medicine*, Vol. 1, No. 2, 2011, pp. 303–312.

Wong, Eunice C., Rebecca L. Collins, and Jennifer Cerully, *Reviewing the Evidence Base for Mental Health First Aid: Is There Support for Its Use with Key Target Populations in California?* Santa Monica, Calif.: RAND Corporation, RR-972-CMHSA, 2015. As of February 13, 2018: https://www.rand.org/pubs/research_reports/RR972.html

Zimering, Rose, Suzy B. Gulliver, Jeffrey Knight, James Munroe, and Terence M. Keane, "Posttraumatic Stress Disorder in Disaster Relief Workers Following Direct and Indirect Trauma Exposure to Ground Zero," *Journal of Traumatic Stress*, Vol. 19, No. 4, August 2006, pp. 553–557.